G000081163

SAKI'S PLAYS

Saki's Plays

'The Death Trap', 'Karl-Ludwig's Window',
'The Miracle Merchant' & 'The Watched Pot'

RENARD PRESS

RENARD PRESS LTD

Kemp House
152–160 City Road
London EC1V 2NX
United Kingdom
info@renardpress.com
020 8050 2928

www.renardpress.com

'The Death Trap', 'Karl-Ludwig's Window' and 'The Watched Pot' first published in *The Square Egg and Other Sketches* in 1924
'The Miracle Merchant' first published in *One-Act Plays for Stage and Study* in 1934
This edition first published by Renard Press Ltd in 2022

Edited text, notes and Biographical Note © Renard Press Ltd, 2022

Cover design by Will Dady

Printed in the United Kingdom by Severn

ISBN: 978-1-913724-69-6

9 8 7 6 5 4 3 2 1

Renard Press is proud to be a carbon positive publisher, meaning we remove more carbon from the air than we emit. For more information see renardpress.com/eco.

All rights reserved. This publication may not be reproduced, stored in a retrieval system or transmitted, in any form or by any means – electronic, mechanical, photocopying, recording or otherwise – without the prior permission of the publisher.

CONTENTS

SAKI'S PLAYS

'The Death Trap', 'Karl-Ludwig's Window',
'The Miracle Merchant' & The Watched Pot'

THE DEATH TRAP

CHARACTERS

DIMITRI, *reigning prince of Kedaria*
DR STRONETZ
COLONEL GIRNITZA, MAJOR VONTIEFF
and CAPTAIN SHULTZ, *officers of the*
Kranitzki Regiment of Guards

Scene
An antechamber in the Prince's castle at Tzern

Time
The present day. The scene opens about
ten o'clock in the evening.

SCENE

An antechamber, rather sparsely furnished. Some rugs of Balkan manufacture on the walls. A narrow table in centre of room; another table set with wine bottles and goblets near window, right. Some high-backed chairs set here and there round room. Tiled stove, left; door in centre.

GIRNITZA, VONTIEFF and SHULTZ are talking together as curtain rises.

GIRNITZA: The prince suspects something – I can see it in his manner.

SHULTZ: Let him suspect. He will know for certain in an half hour's time.

GIRNITZA: The moment the Andrieff Regiment has marched out of the town we are ready for him.

SHULTZ (*drawing revolver from case and aiming it at an imaginary person*): And then... short shrift for Your Royal Highness! I don't think many of my bullets will go astray.

GIRNITZA: The revolver was never a favourite weapon of mine. (*Half-drawing his sword and sending it back into its scabbard with a click:*) I shall finish the job with this.

VONTIEFF: Oh, we shall do for him, right enough. It's a pity he's such a boy, though. I would rather we had a grown man to deal with.

GIRNITZA: We must take our chance when we can find it. Grown men marry and breed heirs, and then one has to massacre a whole family. When we have killed this boy we have killed the last of the dynasty, and laid the way clear for Prince Karl. As long as there was one of this brood left our good Karl could never win the throne.

VONTIEFF: Oh, I know this is our great chance. Still, I wish the boy could be cleared out of our path by the finger of Heaven rather than by our hands.

SHULTZ: Hush! Here he comes.

(Enter, by door, centre, PRINCE DIMITRI, in undress cavalry uniform. He comes straight into room, begins taking cigarette out of a case and looks coldly at the three OFFICERS.)

DIMITRI: You needn't wait.

(They bow and withdraw, SHULTZ going last and staring insolently at the PRINCE, who seats himself at table, centre. As door shuts he stares for a moment at it, then suddenly bows his head on his arms in attitude of despair. A knock is heard at the door. DIMITRI leaps to his feet. Enter STRONETZ, in civilian attire.)

DIMITRI *(eagerly)*: Stronetz! My God, how glad I am to see you!

STRONETZ: One wouldn't have thought so, judging by the difficulty I had in gaining admission. I had to invent a

12

special order to see you on a matter of health. And they made me give up my revolver – they said it was some new regulation.

DIMITRI (*with a short laugh*): They have taken away every weapon I possess under some pretext or another. My sword has gone to be reset, my revolver is being cleaned, my hunting knife has been mislaid...

STRONETZ (*horrified*): My God, Dimitri! You don't mean...?

DIMITRI: Yes, I do. I am trapped. Since I came to the throne three years ago as a boy of fourteen I have been watched and guarded against this moment, but it has caught me unawares.

STRONETZ: But your guards!

DIMITRI: Did you notice the uniforms? The Kranitzki Regiment. They are heart and soul for Prince Karl; the artillery are equally disaffected. The Andrieff Regiment was the only doubtful factor in their plans, and it marches out to camp tonight. The Lonyadi Regiment comes in to relieve it an hour or so later.

STRONETZ: They are loyal, surely?

DIMITRI: Yes, but their loyalty will arrive an hour or so too late.

STRONETZ: Dimitri! You mustn't stay here to be killed! You must get out quick!

DIMITRI: My dear good Stronetz, for more than a generation the Karl faction have been trying to stamp our line out of existence. I am the last of the lot – do you suppose that they are going to let me slip out of their claws now? They're not so damned silly.

STRONETZ: But this is awful! You sit there and talk as if it were a move in a chess game.

DIMITRI (*rising*): Oh, Stronetz! If you knew how I hate death! I'm not a coward, but I do so want to live. Life is so horribly fascinating when one is young, and I've tasted so little of it yet. (*Goes to window.*) Look out of the window at that fairyland of mountains with the forest running up and down all over it. You can just see Grodvitz, where I shot all last autumn, up there on the left, and far away beyond it all is Vienna. Were you ever in Vienna, Stronetz? I've only been there once, and it seemed like a magic city to me. And there are other wonderful cities in the world that I've never seen. Oh, I do so want to live. Think of it: here I am alive and talking to you, as we've talked dozens of times in this grey old room, and tomorrow a fat stupid servant will be washing up a red stain in that corner – I think it will probably be in that corner. (*He points to corner near stove, left.*)

STRONETZ: But you mustn't be butchered in cold blood like this, Dimitri. If they've left you nothing to fight with I can give you a drug from my case that will bring you a speedy death before they can touch you.

DIMITRI: Thanks, no, old chap. You had better leave before it begins – they won't touch you. But I won't drug myself. I've never seen anyone killed before, and I shan't get another opportunity.

STRONETZ: Then I won't leave you; you can see two men killed while you are about it.

(*A band is heard in distance playing a march.*)

14

DIMITRI: The Andrieff Regiment marching out! Now they won't waste much time! (*He draws himself up tense in corner by stove.*) Hush, they are coming!

STRONETZ (*rushing suddenly towards* DIMITRI): Quick! An idea! Tear open your tunic!

(*He unfastens* DIMITRI'*s tunic and appears to be testing his heart. The door swings open and the three* OFFICERS *enter.* STRONETZ *waves a hand commanding silence, and continues his testing. The* OFFICERS *stare at him.*)

GIRNITZA: Dr Stronetz, will you have the goodness to leave the room? We have some business with His Royal Highness. Urgent business, Dr Stronetz.

STRONETZ (*facing round*): Gentlemen, I fear that my business is more grave. I have the saddest of duties to perform. I know you would all gladly lay down your lives for your prince, but there are some perils which even your courage cannot avert.

GIRNITZA (*puzzled*): What are talking of, sir?

STRONETZ: The prince sent for me to prescribe for some disquieting symptoms that have declared themselves. I have made my examination. My duty is a cruel one… I cannot give him six days to live!

(DIMITRI *sinks into chair near table in pretended collapse. The* OFFICERS *turn to each other, nonplussed.*)

GIRNITZA: You are certain? It is a grave thing you are saying. You are not making any mistake?

15

STRONETZ: (*laying his hand on* DIMITRI's *shoulder*): Would to God I were!

(*The* OFFICERS *again turn, whispering to each other.*)

GIRNITZA: It seems our business can wait.
VONTIEFF (*to* DIMITRI): Sire, this is the finger of Heaven.
DIMITRI (*brokenly*): Leave me.

(*They salute and slowly withdraw.* DIMITRI *slowly raises his head, then springs to his feet, rushes to door and listens, then turns round jubilantly to* STRONETZ.)

DIMITRI: Spoofed them! Ye gods, that was an idea, Stronetz!
STRONETZ (*standing quietly looking at* DIMITRI): It was not altogether an inspiration, Dimitri. A look in your eyes suggested it. I had seen men who were stricken with a mortal disease look like that.
DIMITRI: Never mind what suggested it — you have saved me. The Lonyadi Regiment will be here at any moment, and Girnitza's gang daren't risk anything then. You've fooled them, Stronetz, you've fooled them!
STRONETZ (*sadly*): Boy, I haven't fooled them...

(DIMITRI *stares at him for a long moment.*)

It was a real examination I made while those brutes were waiting there to kill you. It was a real report I made; the malady is there.
DIMITRI (*slowly*): Was it *all* true, what you told them?
STRONETZ: It was all true. You have not six days to live.

DIMITRI (*bitterly*): Death has come twice to me in one evening. I'm afraid he must be in earnest. (*Passionately*:) Why didn't you let them kill me? That would have been better than this 'to be left till called for' business. (*Paces across to window, right, and looks out. Turns suddenly.*) Stronetz! You offered me a way of escape from a cruel death just now. Let me escape now from a crueller one. I am a monarch. I won't be kept waiting by death. Give me that little bottle.

(STRONETZ *hesitates, then draws out a small case, extracts bottle and gives it to him.*)

STRONETZ: Four or five drops will do what you ask for.
DIMITRI: Thank you. And now, old friend, goodbye. Go quickly: you've seen me just a little brave – I may not keep it up. I want you to remember me as being brave. Goodbye, best of friends; go.

(STRONETZ *wrings his hand and rushes from the room with his face hidden in his arm. The door shuts.* DIMITRI *looks for a moment after his friend. Then he goes quickly over to side table and uncorks wine bottle. He is about to pour some wine into a goblet when he pauses, as if struck by a new idea. He goes to door, throws it open and listens, then calls out.*

DIMITRI: Girnitza, Vontieff, Shultz!

(*Darting back to the table he pours the entire phial of poison into the wine bottle, and thrusts phial into his pocket. Enter the three* OFFICERS.)

(*Pouring the wine into four goblets:*) The Prince is dead – long live the Prince! (*He seats himself.*) The old feud must be healed now – there is no one left of my family to keep it on; Prince Karl must succeed. Long life to Prince Karl! Gentlemen of the Kranitzki Guard, drink to your future sovereign.

(*The three* OFFICERS *drink, after glancing at each other.*)

GIRNITZA: Sire, we shall never serve a more gallant prince than Your Royal Highness.

DIMITRI: That is true, because you will never serve another prince. Observe, I drink fair! (*Drains goblet.*)

GIRNITZA: What do you mean, 'never serve another prince'?

DIMITRI (*rises*): I mean that I am going to march into the next world at the head of my Kranitzki Guards. You came in here tonight to kill me. You found that death had forestalled you. I thought it a pity that the evening should be wasted, so I've killed *you*, that's all!

SHULTZ: The wine! He's poisoned us!

(VONTIEFF *seizes the bottle and examines it.* SHULTZ *smells his empty goblet.*)

GIRNITZA: Ah! Poisoned! (*He draws his sword and makes a step towards* DIMITRI, *who is sitting on the edge of the centre table.*)

DIMITRI: Oh, certainly, if you wish it. I'm due to die of disease in a few days and of poison in a minute or two, but if you like to take a little extra trouble about my end, please yourself.

(GIRNITZA *reels and drops sword on table and falls back into chair groaning.* SHULTZ *falls across table and* VONTIEFF *staggers against wall. At that moment a lively march is heard approaching.* DIMITRI *seizes the sword and waves it.*)

Aha! The Lonyadi Regiment marching in! My good loyal Kranitzki Guards shall keep me company into the next world. God save the Prince! (*Laughs wildly.*) Colonel Girnitza, I never thought death... could be... so amusing. (*He falls, dying, to the ground.*)

CURTAIN

KARL-LUDWIG'S WINDOW

A Drama in One Act

CHARACTERS

KURT VON JAGDSTEIN
THE GRÄFIN VON JAGDSTEIN, *his mother**

Guests at the Schloss Jagdstein:
ISADORA, *his betrothed*
PHILIP, ISADORA*'s brother*
VIKTORIA, *niece of the* GRÄFIN
BARON RABEL, *a parvenu**

AN OFFICER

Scene
Karl-Ludwig's room in the Schloss Jagdstein, on the
outskirts of a town in eastern Europe

Time
An evening in Carnival Week, the present day

SCENE

A room furnished in medieval style. In the centre a massive tiled stove of old German pattern, over which, on a broad shelf, a large clock. Above the clock a painting of a man in sixteenth-century costume. Immediately to left, in a deep embrasure, a window with a high window seat. Immediately on right of stove an old iron-clamped door, approached by two steps. The walls to left and right are hung with faded tapestry. In the foreground a long oak table, with chairs right, left and centre, and a low armchair on left of stage. On the table are high-stemmed goblets and wine bottles, and a decanter of cognac with some smaller glasses.

THE GRÄFIN, *in an old Court costume, and* BARON RABEL, *also in some Court attire of a bygone age, are discovered. Both wear little black velvet masks.* THE BARON *bows low to the lady, who makes him a mock curtsy. They remove their masks.*

GRÄFIN (*seating herself at left of table*): Of course we old birds are the first to be ready. Light a cigar, Baron, and make yourself at your ease while the young folks are completing their costumes.

BARON (*seating himself at table*): At my ease in this room I could never be. It makes my flesh creep every time I enter it. I am what the world calls a parvenu (*lights cigar*) – a man of today, or perhaps I should say of this afternoon – while your family is of the day before yesterday and many yesterdays before that. Naturally I envy you your ancestry, your title, your position, but there is one thing I do not envy you.

GRÄFIN (*helping herself to wine*): And that is…?

BARON: Your horrible creepy traditions.

GRÄFIN: You mean Karl-Ludwig, I suppose? Yes, this room is certainly full of his associations. There is his portrait, and there is the window from which he was flung down. Only, it is more than a tradition – it really happened.

BARON: That makes it all the more horrible. I am a man who belongs to a milder age, and it sickens me to think of the brutal deed that was carried through in this room. How his enemies stole in upon him and took him unawares, and how they dragged him screaming to that dreadful window.

GRÄFIN: Not screaming, I hope – cursing and storming, perhaps. I don't think a Von Jagdstein would scream even in a moment like that.

BARON: The bravest man's courage might be turned to water looking down at death from that horrid window. It makes one's breath go, even to look down in safety; one can see the stones of the courtyard fathoms and fathoms below.

GRÄFIN: Let us hope he hadn't time to think about it. It would be the thinking of it that would be so terrible.

BARON (*with a shudder*): Ah, indeed! I assure you the glimpse down from that window has haunted me ever since I looked.

GRÄFIN: The window is not the only thing in the room that is haunted. They say that whenever one of the family

24

is going to die a violent death that door swings open and shuts again of its own accord. It is supposed to be Karl-Ludwig's ghost coming in.

BARON (*with apprehensive glance behind him*): What an unpleasant room! Let us forget its associations and talk about something more cheerful. How charming Fräulein Isadora is looking tonight. It is a pity her betrothed could not get leave to come to the ball with her. She is going as Elsa, is she not?

GRÄFIN: Something of the sort, I believe. She's told me so often that I've forgotten.

BARON: You will be fortunate in securing such a daughter-in-law, is it not so?

GRÄFIN: Yes, Isadora has all the most desirable qualifications: heaps of money, average good looks, and absolutely no brains.

BARON: And are the young people very devoted to each other?

GRÄFIN: I am a woman of the world, Baron, and I don't put too high a value on the sentimental side of things, but even I have never seen an engaged couple who made less pretence of caring for one another. Kurt has always been the naughty boy of the family, but he made surprisingly little fuss about being betrothed to Isadora. He said he should never marry anyone he loved, so it didn't matter whom I married him to.

BARON: That was at least accommodating.

GRÄFIN: Besides the financial advantages of the match, the girl's aunt has a very influential position, so for a younger son Kurt is doing rather well.

BARON: He is a clever boy, is he not?

GRÄFIN: He has that perverse kind of cleverness that is infinitely more troublesome than any amount of stupidity. I prefer a fool like Isadora. You can tell beforehand exactly what she will say or do under any given circumstances, exactly on what days she will have a headache, and exactly how many garments she will send to the wash on Mondays.

BARON: A most convenient temperament.

GRÄFIN: With Kurt one never knows where one is. Now, being in the same regiment with the Archduke ought to be of some advantage to him in his career, if he plays his cards well. But of course he'll do nothing of the sort.

BARON: Perhaps the fact of being betrothed will work a change in him.

GRÄFIN: You are an optimist. Nothing ever changes a perverse disposition. Kurt has always been a jarring element in our family circle, but I don't regard one unsatisfactory son out of three as a bad average. It's usually higher.

(*Enter* ISADORA, *dressed as Elsa, followed by* PHILIP, *a blond loutish youth, in the costume of a page, Henry III period.**)

ISADORA: I hope we haven't kept you waiting. I've been helping Viktoria; she'll be here presently.

(*They sit at table.* PHILIP *helps himself to wine.*)

GRÄFIN: We mustn't wait much longer; it's nearly half-past eight now.

BARON: I've just been saying, what a pity the young Kurt could not be here this evening for the ball.

ISADORA: Yes, it is a pity. He is only a few miles away with his regiment, but he can't get leave till the end of the week. It is a pity, isn't it?

GRÄFIN: It is always the way: when one particularly wants people they can never get away.

ISADORA: It's always the way, isn't it?

GRÄFIN: As for Kurt, he has a perfect gift for never being where you want him.

(*Enter* KURT, *in undress cavalry uniform. He comes rapidly into the room.*)

GRÄFIN (*rising with the others*): Kurt! How come you to be here? I thought you couldn't get leave.

(KURT *kisses his mother's hand, then that of* ISADORA, *and bows to the two men.*)

KURT (*pouring out a glass of wine*): I came away in a hurry to avoid arrest. Your health, everybody. (*Drains glass thirstily.*)

GRÄFIN: To avoid arrest!

BARON: Arrest!

(KURT *throws himself wearily into armchair, left of stage. The others stand staring at him.*)

GRÄFIN: What *do* you mean? Arrest for what?

KURT (*quietly*): I have killed the Archduke.*

GRÄFIN: Killed the Archduke! Do you mean you have murdered him?

KURT: Scarcely that – it was a fair duel.

GRÄFIN (*wringing her hands*): Killed the Archduke in a duel? What an unheard-of scandal! Oh, we are ruined!

BARON (*throwing his arms about*): It is unbelievable! What in Heaven's name were the seconds about to let such a thing happen?

KURT (*shortly*): There were no seconds.

GRÄFIN: No seconds? An irregular duel? Worse and worse! What a scandal! What an appalling scandal!

BARON: But how do you mean – no seconds?

KURT: It was in the highest degree desirable that there should be no seconds, so that if the Archduke fell there would be no witnesses to know the why and wherefore of the duel. Of course there will be a scandal, but it will be a sealed scandal.

GRÄFIN: Our poor family! We are ruined.

BARON (*persistently*): But *you* are alive. You will have to give an account of what happened.

KURT: There is only one way in which my account can be rendered.

BARON (*after staring fixedly at him*): You mean...?

KURT (*quietly*): Yes. I escaped arrest only by giving my parole* to follow the Archduke into the next world as soon as might be.

GRÄFIN: A suicide in our family? What an appalling affair! People will never stop talking about it.

ISADORA: It's very unfortunate, isn't it?

GRÄFIN (*crossing over to* ISADORA): My poor child!

(ISADORA *dabs at her eyes. Enter* VIKTORIA, *dressed in Italian peasant costume.*)

28

VIKTORIA: I'm so sorry to be late. All these necklaces took such a time to fasten. Hullo, where did Kurt spring from?

(KURT *rises.*)

GRÄFIN: He has brought some bad news.

VIKTORIA: Oh, how dreadful. Anything very bad? It won't prevent us from going to the ball, will it? It's going to be a particularly gay affair.

(*A faint sound of a tolling bell is heard.*)

KURT: I don't fancy there will be a ball tonight. The news has come as quickly as I have. The bells are tolling already.

BARON (*dramatically*): The scandal is complete!

GRÄFIN: I shall never forgive you, Kurt.

VIKTORIA: But what has happened?

KURT: I should like to say a few words to Isadora. Perhaps you will give us till nine o'clock to talk things over.

GRÄFIN: I suppose it's the proper thing to do under the circumstances. Oh, why should I be afflicted with such a stupid son!

(*Exit the* GRÄFIN, *followed by the* BARON, *who waves his arms about dramatically, and by* PHILIP *and* VIKTORIA. PHILIP *is explaining matters in whispers to the bewildered* VIKTORIA *as they go out.*)

ISADORA (*stupidly*): This is very unfortunate, isn't it?

KURT (*leaning across table with sudden animation as the door closes on the others*): Isadora, I have come to ask you to do something for me. The search party will arrive to arrest me at nine o'clock, and I have given my word that they shall not find me alive. I've got less than twenty minutes left. You *must* promise to do what I ask you.

ISADORA: What is it?

KURT: I suppose it's a strange thing to ask of a woman I'm betrothed to, but there's really no one else who can do it for me. I want you to take a message to the woman I love.

ISADORA: Kurt!

KURT: Of course it's not very conventional, but I knew her and loved her long before I met you – ever since I was eighteen. That's only three years ago, but it seems the greater part of my life. It was a lonely and unhappy life, I remember, till she befriended me, and then it was like the magic of some old fairy tale.

ISADORA: Do I know who she is?

KURT: You must have guessed that long ago. Your aunt will easily be able to get you an opportunity for speaking to her, and you must mention no name, give no token. Just say 'I have a message for you.' She will know who it comes from.

ISADORA: I shall be dreadfully frightened. What is the message?

KURT: Just one word: 'Goodbye.'

ISADORA: It's a very short message, isn't it?

KURT: It's the longest message one heart ever sent to another. Other messages may fade away in the memory, but Time will keep on repeating that message as long as

memory lasts. Every sunset and every nightfall will say
goodbye for me.

(*The door swings open, and then slowly closes of its own accord.*
KURT *represses a shiver.*)

ISADORA (*in a startled voice*): What was that? Who opened
the door?

KURT: Oh, it's nothing. It does that sometimes when...
when... under circumstances like the present. They say
it's old Karl-Ludwig coming in.

ISADORA: I shall faint!

KURT (*in an agonised voice*): Don't you do anything of the sort!
We haven't time for that. You haven't given me your
promise – oh, do make haste. Promise you'll give the
message! (*He seizes both her hands.*)

ISADORA: I promise.

KURT: (*kissing her hands*) Thank you. (*With a change to a lighter
tone:*) I say, you haven't got a loaded revolver on you,
have you? I came away in such a hurry I forgot to bring
one.

ISADORA: Of course I haven't. One doesn't take loaded
revolvers to a masquerade ball.

KURT: It must be Karl-Ludwig's window, then. (*He unbuckles
his sword and throws it into the armchair.*) Oh, I forgot. This
miniature mustn't be found on me. Don't be scandalised
if I do a little undressing. (*He picks up an illustrated paper
from a stool near stove and gives it to* ISADORA *to hold open
in front of her.*) Here you are. (*He proceeds to unbutton his
tunic at the neck and breast and removes a miniature which
is hung round his neck. He gazes at it for a moment, kisses*

31

it, gazes again, then drops it on the floor and grinds it to pieces with his heel. Then he goes to window, opens it and looks down.) I wish the night were darker; one can see right down to the flagstones of the courtyard. It looks awful, but it will look fifty times more horrible in eight minutes' time. (*He comes back to table and seats himself on its edge.*) As I rode along on the way here it seemed such an easy thing to die, and now it's come so close I feel sick with fear. Fancy a Von Jagdstein turning coward. What a scandal, as my dear mother would say. (*He tries to pour out some brandy, but his hand shakes too much.*) Do you mind pouring me out some brandy? I can't steady my hand.

(ISADORA *fills a glass for him.*)

Thanks. No (*pushing it away*), I won't take it; if I can't have my own courage I won't have that kind. But I wish I hadn't looked down just now. Don't you know what it feels like to go down too quickly in a lift, as if one was racing one's inside and winning by a neck? That's what it will feel like for the first second, and then...

(*He hides his eyes a moment in his hands.* ISADORA *falls back in her chair in a faint.* KURT *looks up suddenly at clock.*)

Isadora! Say that the clock is a minute fast! (*He looks towards her.*) She's fainted. Just what she would do. She isn't a brilliant conversationalist, but she was someone to talk to. How beastly lonely it feels up here. Not a soul to say, 'Buck up, Kurt, old boy!' Nothing but a fainting woman and Karl-Ludwig's ghost. I wonder if his ghost is watching me now. I wonder if I shall haunt this room. What a rum idea. (*Looks again at clock and gives a start.*) I *can't* die in three minutes' time. O, God! I can't do it. It isn't the jump that I shrink from now – it's the ending of everything. It's too horrible to think of. To have no more life! Isadora and the Baron and millions of stupid people will go on living, every day will bring them something new, and I shall never have one morsel of life after these three minutes. I *can't* do it. (*Falls heavily into chair, left of table.*) I'll go away somewhere where no one knows me; that will be as good as dying. I told them they should not find me here alive. Well, I can slip away before they come.

(*He rises and moves towards door; his foot grinds on a piece of the broken miniature. He stoops and picks it up, looks hard and long at it, then drops it through his fingers. He turns his head slowly towards the clock and stands watching it. He takes handkerchief from his sleeve and wipes his mouth, returns handkerchief to sleeve, still watching the clock. Some seconds pass in silence... The clock strikes the first stroke of nine.* KURT *turns and walks to the window. He mounts the window seat and stands with one foot on the sill, and looks out and down. He makes the sign of the cross... throws up his arms and jumps into space. The door opens and the* GRÄFIN *enters, followed by an* OFFICER. *They look at the swooning* ISADORA, *then round the room for* KURT.)

33

GRÄFIN: He is gone!

OFFICER: He gave me his word that I should find him here at nine o'clock, and that I should come too late to arrest him. It seems he has tricked me!

GRÄFIN: A Von Jagdstein always keeps his word.

(She stares fixedly at the open window. The OFFICER follows the direction of her gaze, goes over to window, looks out and down. He turns back to the room, straightens himself and salutes.)

CURTAIN

THE MIRACLE MERCHANT

CHARACTERS

MRS BEAUWHISTLE
LOUIS COURCET, *her nephew*
JANE MARTLET
STURRIDGE, MRS BEAUWHISTLE*'s butler*
PAGEBOY

SCENE

Hall-sitting room in MRS BEAUWHISTLE's *country house. French window right. Doors right centre and mid-centre. Staircase left centre. Door left. Long table centre of stage, towards footlights, set with breakfast service. Chairs at table. Writing table and chair right of stage. Small hall table back of stage. Wooden panelling below staircase hung with swords, daggers, etc., in view of audience. Stand with golf clubs, etc. left.*

MRS BEAUWHISTLE seated at writing table; she has had her breakfast. Enter LOUIS down staircase.

LOUIS: Good morning, Aunt. (*He inspects the breakfast dishes.*)
MRS BEAUWHISTLE: Good morning, Louis.
LOUIS: Where is Miss Martlet? (*Helps himself from a dish.*)
MRS BEAUWHISTLE: She finished her breakfast a moment ago.
LOUIS (*sits down*): I'm glad we're alone. I wanted to ask you—

(*Enter STURRIDGE, left, with coffee, which he places on table and withdraws.*)

I wanted to ask you—

MRS BEAUWHISTLE: Whether I could lend you twenty pounds, I suppose?

LOUIS: As a matter of fact, I was only going to ask for fifteen. Perhaps twenty would sound better.

MRS BEAUWHISTLE: The answer is the same, in either case, and it's 'No.' I couldn't even lend you five. You see, I've had no end of extra expenses just lately—

LOUIS: My dear aunt, please don't give reasons. A charming woman should always be unreasonable – it's part of her charm. Just say, 'Louis, I love you very much, but I'm damned if I lend you any more money!' I should understand perfectly.

MRS BEAUWHISTLE: Well, we'll take it as said. I've just had a letter from Dora Bittholz to say she is coming on Thursday.

LOUIS: This next Thursday? I say, that's rather awkward, isn't it?

MRS BEAUWHISTLE: Why awkward?

LOUIS: Jane Martlet has only been here six days, and she never stays less than a fortnight, even when she's asked definitely for a week. You'll never get her out of the house by Thursday.

MRS BEAUWHISTLE: But why should I? She and Dora are good friends, aren't they? They used to be.

LOUIS: Used to be, yes – that is what makes them such bitter enemies now. Each feels that she has nursed a viper in her bosom. Nothing fans the flame of human resentment so much as the discovery that one's bosom has been utilised as a snake sanatorium.

MRS BEAUWHISTLE: But why are they enemies? What have they quarrelled about? Some man, I suppose?

LOUIS: No. A hen has come between them.

MRS BEAUWHISTLE: A hen! What hen?

LOUIS: It was a bronze Leghorn,* or some such exotic breed, and Dora sold it to Jane at a rather exotic price. They both go in for poultry breeding, you know.

MRS BEAUWHISTLE: If Jane agreed to give the price I don't see what there was to quarrel about.

LOUIS: Well, you see, the bird turned out to be an abstainer from the egg habit, and I'm told that the letters that passed between the two women were a revelation as to how much abuse could be got on to a sheet of notepaper.

MRS BEAUWHISTLE: How ridiculous! Couldn't some of their friends compose the quarrel?

LOUIS: It would have been rather like composing the storm music of a Wagner opera. Jane was willing to take back some of her most libellous remarks if Dora would take back the hen.

MRS BEAUWHISTLE: And wouldn't she?

LOUIS: Not she. She said that would be owning herself in the wrong, and you know that Dora would never, under any circumstances, own herself in the wrong. She would as soon think of owning a slum property in Whitechapel as do that.

MRS BEAUWHISTLE: It will be a most awkward situation, having them both under my roof at the same time. Do you suppose they won't speak to one another?

LOUIS: On the contrary – the difficulty will be to get them to leave off. Their descriptions of each other's conduct and character have hitherto been governed by the fact that only four ounces of plain speaking can be sent through the post for a penny.

MRS BEAUWHISTLE: What is to be done? I can't put Dora off, I've already postponed her visit once, and nothing short of a miracle would make Jane leave before her self-allotted fortnight is over.

LOUIS: I don't mind trying to supply a miracle at short notice – miracles are rather in my line.

MRS BEAUWHISTLE: My dear Louis, you'll be clever if you get Jane out of this house before Thursday.

LOUIS: I shall not only be clever, I shall be rich; in sheer gratitude you will say to me, 'Louis, I love you more than ever, and here are the twenty pounds we were speaking about.'

(*Enter* JANE, *door centre.*)

JANE: Good morning, Louis.

LOUIS (*rising*): Good morning, Jane.

JANE: Go on with your breakfast; I've had mine, but I'll just have a cup of coffee to keep you company. (*Helps herself.*) Is there any toast left?

LOUIS: Sturridge is bringing some. Here it comes.

(STURRIDGE *enters left with toast rack.* JANE *seats herself and is helped to toast; she takes three pieces.*)

JANE: Isn't there any butter?

STURRIDGE: Your sleeve is in the butter, miss.

JANE: Oh, yes.

(*Helps herself generously. Exit* STURRIDGE *left.*)

MRS BEAUWHISTLE: Jane, dear, I see the Mackenzie–
Hubbard wedding is on Thursday next. St Peter's, Eaton
Square – such a pretty church for weddings. I suppose
you'll be wanting to run away from us to attend it? You
were always such friends with Louisa Hubbard; it would
hardly do for you not to turn up.

JANE: Oh, I'm not going to bother to go all that way for a
silly wedding, much as I like Louisa; I shall go and stay
with her for several weeks after she's come back from
her honeymoon.

(LOUIS *grins across at his aunt.*)

I don't see any honey!

LOUIS: Your other sleeve's in the honey.

JANE: Bother, so it is. (*Helps herself liberally.*)

MRS BEAUWHISTLE: Well, I must leave you and go and do
some gardening. Ring for anything you want, Jane.

JANE: Thank you, I'm all right.

(*Exit* MRS BEAUWHISTLE *by French window right.*)

LOUIS (*pushing back his chair*): Do you mind my smoking?

JANE (*still eating heartily*): Not at all.

(*Enter* STURRIDGE *with tray, left, as if to clear away breakfast
things. Places tray on side table, back centre, and is about to retire.*)

Oh, I say, can have some more hot milk? This is nearly
cold.

(STURRIDGE *takes jug and exits left.* LOUIS *looks fixedly after him. Seats himself near* JANE *and stares solemnly at the floor.*)

LOUIS: Servants are a bit of a nuisance.

JANE: Servants a nuisance! I should think they are! The trouble I have in getting suited you would hardly believe. But I don't see what you have to complain of – your aunt is so wonderfully lucky in her servants. Sturridge, for instance – he's been with her for years, and I'm sure he's a jewel, as butlers go.

LOUIS: That's just the trouble. It's when servants have been with you for years that they become a really serious nuisance. The other sort, the here-today-and-gone-tomorrow lot, don't matter – you've simply got to replace them. It's the stayers and the jewels that are the real worry.

JANE: But if they give satisfaction—

LOUIS: That doesn't prevent them from giving trouble. As it happens, I was particularly thinking of Sturridge when I made the remark about servants being a nuisance.

JANE: The excellent Sturridge, a nuisance? I can't believe it!

LOUIS: I know he is excellent, and my aunt simply couldn't get along without him. But his very excellence has had an effect on him.

JANE: What effect?

LOUIS (*solemnly*): Have you ever considered what it must be like to go on unceasingly doing the correct thing in the correct manner in the same surroundings for the greater part of a lifetime? To know and ordain and superintend exactly what silver and glass and table linen shall be used and set out on what occasions, to have pantry and

42

cellar and plate cupboard under a minutely devised and undeviating administration, to be noiseless, impalpable, omnipresent, infallible?

JANE (*with conviction*): I should go mad.

LOUIS: Exactly. Mad.

(*Enter* STURRIDGE *left with milk jug, which he places on table and exits left.*)

JANE: But – Sturridge hasn't gone mad.

LOUIS: On most points he's thoroughly sane and reliable, but at times he is subject to the most obstinate delusions.

JANE: Delusions? What sort of delusions? (*She helps herself to more coffee.*)

LOUIS: Unfortunately they usually centre round someone staying in the house – that is where the awkwardness comes in. For instance, he took it into his head that Matilda Sheringham, who was here last summer, was the prophet Elijah.

JANE: The prophet Elijah! The man who was fed by ravens?*

LOUIS: Yes, it was the ravens that particularly impressed Sturridge's imagination. He was rather offended, it seems, at the idea that Matilda should have her private catering arrangements, and he declined to compete with the birds in any way; he wouldn't allow any tea to be sent up to her in the morning, and when he waited at table he passed her over altogether in handing round the dishes. Poor Matilda could scarcely get anything to eat.

JANE: How horrible! How very horrible! Whatever did you do?

LOUIS: It was judged best for her to cut her visit short. (*With emphasis:*) In a case of that kind it was the only thing to be done.

JANE: I shouldn't have done that. (*Cuts herself some bread and butters it.*) I should have humoured him in some way. I should have said the ravens were moulting. I certainly shouldn't have gone away.

LOUIS: It's not always wise to humour people when they get these ideas into their heads. There's no knowing to what lengths they might go.

JANE: You don't mean to say Sturridge might be dangerous?

LOUIS: One can never be certain. Now and then he gets some idea about a guest that might take an unfortunate turn. That is what is worrying me at the present moment.

JANE (*excitedly*): Why, has he taken some fancy about me?

LOUIS (*who has taken a putter out of the stand, left, and is polishing it with an oil rag*): He has.

JANE: No, really? Who on earth does he think I am?

LOUIS: Queen Anne.

JANE: Queen Anne? What an idea! But anyhow, there's nothing dangerous about her; she's such a colourless personality. No one could feel very strongly about Queen Anne.*

LOUIS (*sternly*): What does posterity chiefly say about her?

JANE: The only thing I can remember about her is the saying 'Queen Anne's dead.'*

LOUIS: Exactly. Dead.

JANE: Do you mean that he takes me for the *ghost* of Queen Anne?

LOUIS: Ghost? Dear, no! Who ever heard of a ghost that came down to breakfast and ate kidneys and toast and honey with a healthy appetite? No, it's the fact of you being so very much alive and flourishing that perplexes and irritates him.

JANE (*anxiously*): Irritates him?

LOUIS: Yes. All his life he has been accustomed to look on Queen Anne as the personification of everything that is dead and done with – 'as dead as Queen Anne', you know – and now he has to fill your glass at lunch and dinner and listen to your accounts of the gay time you had at the Dublin Horse Show, and naturally he feels that there is something scandalously wrong somewhere.

JANE (*with increased anxiety*): But he wouldn't be downright hostile to me on that account, would he? Not violent?

LOUIS (*carelessly*): I didn't get really alarmed about it till last night, when he was bringing in the coffee. I caught him scowling at you with a very threatening look and muttering things about you.

JANE: What things?

LOUIS: That you ought to be dead long ago, and that someone should see to it, and that if no one else did he would. (*Cheerfully:*) That's why I mentioned the matter to you.

JANE: This is awful! Your aunt must be told about it at once.

LOUIS: My aunt mustn't hear a word about it. It would upset her dreadfully. She relies on Sturridge for everything.

JANE: But he might kill me at any moment!

LOUIS: Not at any moment – he's busy with the silver all the afternoon.

JANE: What a frightful situation to be in, with a mad butler dangling over one's head.

LOUIS: Of course, it's only a temporary madness; perhaps if you were to cut your visit short and come to us some time later in the year he might have forgotten all about Queen Anne.

JANE: Nothing would induce me to cut short my visit. You must keep a sharp lookout on Sturridge, and be ready to intervene if he gets violent. Probably we are both exaggerating things a bit. (*Rising.*) I must go and write some letters in the morning room. Mind, keep an eye on the man. (*Exit, door right centre.*)

LOUIS (*savagely*): *Quel type!**

(*Enter* MRS BEAUWHISTLE *by French window, right.*)

MRS BEAUWHISTLE: Can't find my gardening gloves anywhere. I suppose they are where I left them; it's a way my things have. (*Rummages in drawer of table, back centre.*) They are. (*Produces gloves from drawer.*) And how is your miracle doing, Louis?

LOUIS: Rotten! I've invented all sorts of excellent reasons for stimulating the migration instinct in that woman, but you might as well try to drive away an attack of indigestion by talking to it.

MRS BEAUWHISTLE: Poor Louis! I'm afraid Jane's staying powers are superior to any amount of hustling that you can bring to bear.

(*Enter* STURRIDGE *left; he begins clearing breakfast things.*)

I could have told you from the first that you were engaged on a wild goose chase.

LOUIS: Chase! You can't chase a thing that refuses to budge. One of the first conditions of the chase is that the thing you are chasing should run away.

MRS BEAUWHISTLE (*laughing*): That's a condition that Jane will never fulfil.

(MRS BEAUWHISTLE *exits through window right.* LOUIS *continues cleaning golf club, then suddenly stops and looks reflectively at* STURRIDGE, *who is busy with the breakfast things.*)

LOUIS: Where is Miss Martlet?

STURRIDGE: In the morning room, I believe, sir, writing letters.

LOUIS: You see that old basket-hilted sword on the wall?

STURRIDGE: Yes, sir. This big one? (*Points to sword.*)

LOUIS: Miss Martlet wants to copy the inscription on its blade. I wish you would take it to her – my hands are all over oil.

STURRIDGE: Yes, sir. (*Turns to wall where sword is hanging.*)

LOUIS: Take it without the sheath – it will be less trouble.

(STURRIDGE *draws the blade, which is broad and bright, and exits by door centre.* LOUIS *stands back under shadow of staircase. Enter* JANE, *door right centre, at full run.*)

JANE (*screaming*): 'Louis! Louis! Where are you?'

(JANE *rushes up stairs at top speed. Enter* STURRIDGE *door right centre, sword in hand.* LOUIS *steps forward.*)

STURRIDGE: Miss Martlet slipped out of the room, sir, as I came in – I don't think she saw me coming. Seemed in a bit of a hurry.

LOUIS: Perhaps she has a train to catch. Never mind, you can put the sword back. I'll copy out the inscription for her later.

(STURRIDGE *returns sword to its place.* LOUIS *continues cleaning putter.* STURRIDGE *carries breakfast tray out by door left. Enter* PAGE, *running full speed down stairs.*)

PAGE: The timetable! Miss Martlet wants to look up a train.

(LOUIS *dashes to drawer of small table, centre; he and* PAGE *hunt through contents, throwing gloves, etc., on to floor.*)

LOUIS: Here it is!

(PAGE *seizes book, starts to run upstairs;* LOUIS *grabs him by tip of jacket, pulls him back, opens books, searches frantically.*)

Here you are. Leaves eleven fifty-five, arrives Charing Cross two-twenty.

(PAGE *dashes upstairs with timetable.* LOUIS *flies to speaking tube in wall left, whistles down it.*)

Is that you, Tomkins? The car, as quick as you can, to catch the eleven fifty-five. Never mind your livery, just as you are.

(*Shuts off tube.* PAGE *dashes down stairs.*)

PAGE: Miss Martlet's golf clubs!

(LOUIS *dashes for them in stand and gives them to boy.*)

LOUIS: Here, this Tam-o'-shanter is hers – and this motor
  veil. (*Gives them to boy.*)
PAGE: She said there was a novel of hers down here.

(LOUIS *goes to writing table, where there are six books on shelf, and
gives them all to* PAGE.)

LOUIS: Here, take the lot. Fly!

(LOUIS *pushes the* PAGE *vigorously up first steps of staircase.
Exit* PAGE. *The sound of books dropping can be heard as he goes.*
LOUIS *dashes round room to see if anything more belonging to*
JANE *remains. Looks at his watch; compares it with small clock on
writing table. Goes to speaking tube.*)

  Hullo, is Tomkins there? What? Oh, all right. (*Shuts off
  tube. Goes to table where coffee pot still remains and pours out
  cup of coffee; drinks it. Looks again at watch.*)
STURRIDGE (*enters left*): The car has come round, sir.
LOUIS: Good. I'll go and tell Miss Martlet. Will you find my
  aunt – she's somewhere in the garden – and tell her that
  Miss Martlet had to leave in a hurry to catch the eleven
  fifty-five; called away urgently and couldn't stop to say
  goodbye. Matter of life and death.
STURRIDGE: Yes, sir.

(*Exit* STURRIDGE, *door left.* LOUIS *exits up staircase. Enter*
MRS BEAUWHISTLE *by window right. She has a letter in her
hand. She looks in at door, right centre, returns and calls.*)

MRS BEAUWHISTLE: Louis, Louis!

(*Sound of a motor is heard;* LOUIS *rushes in by door left.*)

LOUIS (*excitedly*): How much did you say you'd lend me if I got rid of Jane Martlet?

MRS BEAUWHISTLE: We needn't get rid of her. Dora has just written to say she can't come this month.

(LOUIS *collapses into chair.*)

CURTAIN

THE WATCHED POT

or,

The Mistress of Briony

The circumstances of our writing 'The Watched Pot' were: Mr Frederick Harrison* was very interested in your brother's original 'Watched Pot', but found it unsuitable for the stage, and brought Saki and myself together in the hope that our joint efforts would make it suitable. My share was shortening it, giving it incident and generally adapting it for stage purposes. Saki used to write more as a novelist than a playwright.

He and I used to have many friendly quarrels, as he was so full of witty remarks that it was a cruel business discarding some of his bons mots. We always used to terminate such quarrels by agreeing to use his axed witticisms in our next play... Shortly before the war Saki at last gave in on the question of plot, and we had practically completed an entirely new story, still retaining the characters which he loved so dearly and which were so typical of his brain.

CHARLES MAUDE*

CHARACTERS

TREVOR BAVVEL

HORTENSIA, *Mrs Bavvel, his mother*

LUDOVIC BAVVEL, *his uncle*

RENÉ ST GALL

Guests at Briony:

AGATHA CLIFFORD

CLARE HENESSEY

SYBIL BOMONT

MRS PETER VULPY

STEPHEN SPARROWBY

COLONEL MUTSOME

THE YOUNGEST DRUMMOND BOY

WILLIAM, *pageboy at Briony*

JOHN, *under-butler at Briony.*

Scene

Act I: Briony Manor breakfast room

Act II: Briony Manor hall (the next evening)

Act III: Briony Manor breakfast room (the next morning)

ACT I

Breakfast room at Briony Manor.

LUDOVIC *fidgeting with papers at escritoire,* * *left, occasionally writing.* MRS VULPY *seated in armchair, right, with her back partially turned to him, glancing at illustrated papers.*

MRS VULPY (*with would-be fashionable drawl*): So sweet of your dear cousin Agatha to bring me down here with her. Such a refreshing change from the dust and glare of Folkestone.

LUDOVIC (*absently*): Yes, I suppose so.

MRS VULPY: And so unexpected. Her invitation took me quite by surprise.

LUDOVIC: Dear Agatha is always taking people by surprise. She was born taking people by surprise; in Goodwood Week,* I believe, with an ambassador staying in the house who hated babies. So thoroughly like her. One feels certain that she'll die one of these days in some surprising and highly inconvenient manner – probably from snakebite on the Terrace of the House of Commons.

MRS VULPY: I'm afraid you don't like your cousin.

LUDOVIC: Oh, dear, yes. I make it a rule to like my relations. I remember only their good qualities and forget their birthdays. (*With increased animation, rising from his seat and approaching her.*) Excuse the question, Mrs Vulpy; are you a widow?

MRS VULPY: I really can't say with any certainty.

LUDOVIC: You can't say?

MRS VULPY: With any certainty. According to latest mail advices from Johannesburg my husband, Mr Peter Vulpy, was not expected by his medical attendants to last into the next week. On the other hand, a cablegram from the local mining organ to a City newspaper over here congratulates that genuine sportsman, Mr P. Vulpy, on his recovery from his recent severe illness. There happens to be a Percival Vulpy in Johannesburg, so my present information is not very conclusive in either direction. Doctors and journalists are both so untrustworthy, aren't they?

LUDOVIC: Could your Mr P. Vulpy be correctly described as a genuine sportsman?

MRS VULPY: There was nothing genuine about Peter. I've never heard of his hitting even a partridge in anger, but he used to wear a horseshoe scarf pin, and I've known him to watch football matches, so I suppose he might be described as a sportsman. For all I know to the contrary, he may by this time have joined the majority, who are powerless to resent these intrusions, but my private impression is that he's sitting up and taking light nourishment in increasing doses.

LUDOVIC: How extremely unsatisfactory.

MRS VULPY: Really, Mr Bavvel, I think if anyone is to mourn Mr Vulpy's continued existence I should be allowed that privilege. After all, he's my husband, you know. Perhaps you are one of those who don't believe that the marriage tie gives one any proprietary rights?

LUDOVIC: Oh, most certainly I do. I am a prospective candidate for Parliamentary honours, and I believe in all the usual things. My objection to Mr Vulpy's inconvenient vitality is entirely impersonal. If you were in a state of widowhood there would be no obstacle to your marrying Trevor. (*Resumes seat at escritoire, but sits facing her.*)

MRS VULPY: Marrying Trevor! Really, this is interesting. And why, pray, should I be singled out for that destiny?

LUDOVIC: My dear Mrs Vulpy, let me be absolutely frank with you. Honoured as we should be to welcome you into the family circle, I may at once confess that my solicitude is not so much to see you married to my nephew as to see him married to somebody – happily and suitably married, of course, but anyhow, married.

MRS VULPY: Indeed!

LUDOVIC: Briefly, the gist of the business is this: like most gifted young men, Trevor has a mother.

MRS VULPY: Oh, I fancy I know *that* already.

LUDOVIC: One could scarcely be at Briony for half an hour without making that discovery.

MRS VULPY: Hortensia, Mrs Bavvel, is not exactly one of those things that one can hide under a damask cheek,* or whatever the saying is.

LUDOVIC: Hortensia is a very estimable woman. Most estimable women are apt to be a little trying. Without pretending to an exhaustive knowledge on the subject,

55

I should say Hortensia was the most trying woman in Somersetshire. Probably without exaggeration one of the most trying women in the West of England. My late brother Edward, Hortensia's husband, who was not given to making original observations if he could find others ready-made to his hand, used to declare that marriage was a lottery. Like most popular sayings, that simile breaks down on application. In a lottery there are prizes and blanks; no one who knew her would think of describing Hortensia as either a prize or a blank.

MRS VULPY: Well, no: she doesn't come comfortably under either heading.

LUDOVIC: My brother was distinguished for what is known as a retiring disposition. Hortensia, on the other hand, was dowered with a commanding personality. Needless to say she became a power in the household – in a very short time the only power; a sort of Governor-General and Mother Superior and political boss rolled into one. A Catherine the Second of Russia* without any of Catherine's redeeming vices.

MRS VULPY: An uncomfortable sort of person to live with.

LUDOVIC: Hortensia did everything that had to be done in the management of a large estate – and a great deal that might have been left undone: she engaged and dismissed gardeners, decided which of the under-gamekeepers might marry and how much gooseberry jam should be made in a given year, regulated the speed at which perambulators might be driven through the village street and the number of candles which might be lit in church on dark afternoons without suspicion of Popery.* Almost the only periodical literature that she

56

allowed in the house was the *Spectator* and the *Exchange and Mart*, neither of which showed any tendency to publish betting news. Halma* and chess were forbidden on Sundays for fear of setting a bad example to the servants.

MRS VULPY: If servants knew how often the fear of leading them astray by bad example holds us back from desperate wickedness, I'm sure they would ask for double wages. And what was poor Mr Edward doing all this time?

LUDOVIC: Edward was not of a complaining disposition, and for a while he endured Hortensia with a certain philosophic calm. Later, however, he gave way to golf.

MRS VULPY: And Hortensia went on bossing things?

LUDOVIC: From the lack of any organised opposition her autocracy rapidly developed into a despotism. Her gubernatorial energies overflowed the limits of the estate and parish, and she became a sort of minor power in the moral and political life of the county, not to say the nation. Nothing seemed to escape her vigilance, whether it happened in the Established Church or the servants' hall or the Foreign Office. She quarrelled with the Macedonian policy* of every successive Government, exposed the hitherto unsuspected atheism of the nearest Dean and Chapter, and dismissed a pageboy for parting his hair in the middle. With equal readiness she prescribed rules for the better management of the Young Women's Christian Association and the Devon and Somerset Staghounds. Briony used to be a favourite rendezvous for the scattered members of the family. Under the Hortensia regime we began to find the train service less convenient and our opportunities for making prolonged visits recurred at rare intervals.

MRS VULPY: Didn't her health wear out under all that strain of activity?

LUDOVIC: With the exception of an occasional full-dress headache, Hortensia enjoyed implacable good health. We resigned ourselves to the prospect of the good lady's rule at Briony for the rest of our natural lives. Then something happened which we had left out of our calculations. Edward caught a chill out otter-hunting and in less than a week Hortensia was a widow. We are what is known as a very united family, and poor dear Edward's death affected us acutely.

MRS VULPY: Naturally it would, coming so suddenly.

LUDOVIC: At the same time, there was a rainbow of consolation irradiating our grief. Edward's otherwise untimely decease seemed to promise the early dethronement of Hortensia. Trevor was twenty years of age, and in the natural course of things he would soon be absolute master of Briony, and the relict* of Edward Bavvel would be denuded of her despotic terrors and become merely a tiresome old woman. As I have said, we were all much attached to poor Edward, but somehow his funeral was one of the most cheerful functions that had been celebrated at Briony for many years. Then came a discovery that cast a genuine gloom over the whole affair. Edward had left the management of the estate and the control of his entire and very considerable fortune to Hortensia until such time as Trevor should take unto himself a wife. (*Rises from seat and takes short steps up and down.*) That was six long years ago, and Trevor

58

is still unmarried, unengaged, not even markedly attracted towards any eligible female. Hortensia, on the other hand, has… well, ripened, without undergoing any process of mellowing; rather the reverse.

MRS VULPY: Aha! I begin to spot the nigger in the timber yard.*

LUDOVIC: I beg your pardon?

MRS VULPY: I begin to twig. Deprived by Trevor's marriage of her control of the moneybags, Hortensia, as a domestic tyrant, would shrink down to bearable limits.

LUDOVIC (*seating himself*): Hortensia under existing circumstances is like a permeating dust storm, which you can't possibly get away from or pretend that it's not there. Living with a comparatively modest establishment at the dower house,* she would be merely like town in August or the bite of a camel – a painful experience which may be avoided with a little ordinary prudence.

MRS VULPY: I don't wonder that you're keen on the change.

LUDOVIC: Keen! There is no one on the estate or in the family who doesn't include it in his or her private litany of daily wants.

MRS VULPY: And I suppose Mrs Bavvel is not at all anxious to see herself put on the shelf, and does her best to head Mr Trevor off from any immediate matrimonial projects?

LUDOVIC: Of course, Hortensia recognises the desirability of Trevor ultimately finding a suitable consort, if only for carrying on the family. I've no doubt that one day she'll produce some flabby little nonentity who will be flung into Trevor's arms with a maternal benediction.

MRS VULPY: Meantime you haven't been able to get him to commit himself in any way. But perhaps his mother would break off any engagement she didn't approve of?

LUDOVIC: Oh, no fear of that. With all his inertness, Trevor has a wholesome strain of obstinacy in his composition. If he once gets engaged to a girl, he'll marry her. The trouble is that his obstinacy takes the form of his refusing to be seriously attracted by any particular competitor. If patient, determined effort on the part of others would have availed he would have been married dozens of times, but a touch of real genius is required. That is why I appeal to you to help us.

MRS VULPY: I suppose Agatha considers herself in the running?

LUDOVIC: Poor Agatha has a perfect genius for supporting lost causes. I've no doubt she fancies she has an off chance of becoming Mrs Trevor Bavvel. I've equally no doubt that she never will. Agatha is one of those unaccountable people who are impelled to keep up an inconsequent flow of conversation if they detect you trying to read a book or write a letter, and if you should be suffering from an acknowledged headache she invariably bangs out something particularly triumphant on the nearest piano by way of showing that she at least is not downhearted. Or if you want to think out some complicated problem she will come and sit by your side and read through an entire bulb catalogue to you, with explanatory comments of her own. No, we are all very fond of Agatha, but strictly as a cheerful inane sort of person to have about the house – someone else's house, for preference.

MRS VULPY: And what about Miss Henessey?

LUDOVIC: Oh, Clare: she's a rattling good sort in her way, and at one time I used to hope that she and Trevor might hit it off. I think in his own sleepy way he was rather attracted to her. Unfortunately, she only pays rare visits here, and even that she has to keep dark. You see, she's the favourite grandniece and prospective heiress of old Mrs Packington – you've heard of Mrs Packington?

MRS VULPY: No; who is she?

LUDOVIC: She lives near Bath, and she's fabulously old, and fabulously rich, and she's been fabulously ill for longer than any living human being can remember. I believe she caught a chill at Queen Victoria's coronation* and never let it go again. The most human thing about her is her dislike for Hortensia, who, I believe, once advised her to take more exercise and less medicine. The old lady has ever since alluded to her as a rattlesnake in dove's plumage, and has more than once, with her dying breath, cautioned Clare against intercourse with Briony and its inhabitants. So you see, there's not much to be hoped for in that direction.

MRS VULPY: Awfully provoking, isn't it? What about Sybil Bomont?

LUDOVIC: Ah, Sybil is the one ray of hope that I can see on the horizon. Personally, she's rather too prickly in her temperament to suit me. She has a fatal gift for detecting the weak spots in her fellow humans and sticking her spikes into them. Matrimony is not reputed to be an invariable bed of roses, but there is no reason why it should be a cactus hedge. However, she is clever enough to keep that side of her character to the wall whenever Trevor is alongside.

MRS VULPY: And you think she's got a good sporting chance with him?

LUDOVIC: She isn't losing any opportunities that come along, and I'm naturally trying my best to drive the game up her way, but the daily round at Briony doesn't give us much help. We begin the day with solid breakfast businesses; then there are partridges to be tramped after, and Trevor takes his birds rather solemnly, as though it hurts him more than it does them, you know. In the evening a solid dinner, and then bridge for such small stakes that even Agatha can't lose enough in a fortnight to convince her that she can't play. Then bed.

MRS VULPY: Well, that's not a very promising programme for anyone who's working a matrimonial movement. Couldn't we get up something that would supply a few more openings? Why not theatricals?

LUDOVIC: Theatricals? At Briony? You might as well suggest a massacre of Christian villagers! Hortensia looks on the stage and everything that pertains to it as a sort of early door to the infernal regions.

MRS VULPY: What about a gymkhana?*

LUDOVIC: Infinitely worse. The mention of a gymkhana would suggest to Hortensia's mind the unchastened restlessness of the Anglo Saxon grafted on to the traditional licentiousness of the purple* East. The very word 'gymkhana' reeks with an aroma of long drinks, sweepstakes and betrayed husbands, and the usual things that are supposed to strew the social horizon east of Suez.

MRS VULPY: Well, I'm afraid it's hopeless. I give it up.

LUDOVIC (*rising hastily from his seat*): Dear Mrs Vulpy, on no account give it up. I rely so much on your tact and insight and experience. You *must* think of something.

I'm not a wealthy man, but if you help me to pull this through I promise you my gratitude shall take concrete shape. A commemorative bracelet, for instance – have you any particular favourite stones?

MRS VULPY: I love all stones – except garnets or moonstones.

LUDOVIC: You think it unlucky to have moonstones?

MRS VULPY: Oh, distinctly, if you've the chance of getting something more valuable. I adore rubies; they're so sympathetic.

LUDOVIC: I'll make a note of it. (*Writes in pocketbook.*)

MRS VULPY: I gather that we're to concentrate on Sybil?

LUDOVIC: Sybil, certainly. And of course, if there's anything I can do to back you up—

(*Enter* CLARE *and* SYBIL *by door, left, back.*)

No, I don't know that part of Switzerland – I once spent a winter at St Moritz.

(CLARE *seats herself on couch, right.* SYBIL *takes chair in centre stage.*)

CLARE: You needn't pretend you're discussing Swiss health resorts, because you're not.

MRS VULPY: Oh, but we are, Miss Henessey. I was just saying Montreux was so—

CLARE: You were discussing Trevor and possible Mrs Trevors. My dear Mrs Vulpy, it's our one subject of discussion here.

SYBIL: It's a frightfully absorbing subject, especially for me.

CLARE: Why for you especially?

SYBIL: Oh, well, dear...

LUDOVIC: We did touch on the subject, I admit, and Mrs
    Vulpy has very kindly offered to help matters along in
    that direction if she can find an opportunity.

SYBIL: Have you had bad news from South Africa?

MRS VULPY: Oh, dear, no. My offer is quite disinterested.

SYBIL: How noble of you. How do you propose to begin?

MRS VULPY: Well, I was just suggesting a little departure
    from the usual routine of life here, something that would
    give an opening for a clever girl to bring a man to the
    scratch. But it seems that Mrs Bavvel is rather against
    any of the more promising forms of entertainment.

SYBIL: We've had the annual harvest thanksgiving, but Trevor
    was seedy and couldn't help with the decorations.

MRS VULPY: Harvest thanksgiving?

CLARE: Yes, it's one of our rural institutions. We get our
    corn and most of our fruit from abroad, but we always
    assemble the local farmers and tenantry to give thanks
    for the harvest. So broad-minded of us. It shows such a
    nice spirit for a Somersetshire farmer to be duly thank-
    ful for the ripening of the Carlsbad plum.

MRS VULPY: Is Mrs Bavvel never absent at dinner parties
    or anything of that sort? A little impromptu frolic is
    sometimes a great success.

LUDOVIC: Now, if you're going to plot anything illicit I must
    really leave you. Hortensia is not in very great demand
    as a dinner guest, but she is taking me tomorrow to a
    meeting at Panfold in connection with the opening of
    a free library there, and there will be a reception of
    some sort in the town hall afterwards. I entirely disap-
    prove of anything of a festive nature taking place here
    behind her back, but... we shan't be home much before

midnight. It's a fairly long drive. Understand? I entirely disapprove. (*Gathers papers and exits, door left front.*)

SYBIL: This threatens to be rather sporting. What have you got up your sleeve?

MRS VULPY: Oh, nothing – only, why not beat up* your men and girlfriends at short notice and have a Cinderella?* There's a lovely floor in the morning room and a good piano, and you could have a scratch supper.

CLARE: And how about the servants? Are we to beg them all individually to hold their tongues about the affair?

MRS VULPY: Oh, of course Mrs Bavvel would have to know about it next day.

CLARE: It's very well for you to talk like that – you're a comparative stranger here, and I dare say you'd find a certain amount of amusement in the situation. Those of us who know what Hortensia is like when anything displeases her... well, it would simply be a case of Bradshaw at breakfast and a tea basket at Yeovil.*

MRS VULPY: But then we're playing to win; it's a sort of coup d'état. With the fun and excitement of the dancing and the music, and of course the sitting-out places, and, above all, the charming sense of doing something wrong, the betting is that Trevor will be engaged to one of you girls before the night's out. And then the morrow can be left to take care of itself.

SYBIL: It sounds *lovely.* I'm horribly frightened of Hortensia, but I'm game to get up this dance.

CLARE: A coup d'état is a wretchedly messy thing. It's as bad as cooking with a chafing dish;* it takes such ages to clean things up afterwards.

(*Enter* AGATHA, *door right back, with two large baskets piled with asters, dahlias, etc., and long trails of ivy and brambles.*)

AGATHA: Hullo, you idle people. I'm just going to arrange the flowers. (*Puts baskets down on escritoire.*)

SYBIL: Are you? Why?

AGATHA: Oh, I always do when I'm here. (*Begins slopping flowers and leaves about in inconvenient places.*)

MRS VULPY: We're plotting to have a little impromptu dance here tomorrow night.

AGATHA (*spilling a lot of dahlias over* MRS VULPY): Oh, you dear things, how delightful! But whatever will Hortensia say?

SYBIL: Hortensia is opening an ear hospital or free library or some such horror at Panfold, and won't know about it till it's all over, and then it will be too late to say much.

CLARE: I fancy you'll find that Hortensia's motto will be 'better late than never'.

AGATHA: Oh, I fancy she'll be rather furious. But what fun, all the same. But who will we get to come?

SYBIL: Oh, we can get nine couples easily. There's all the Abingdon house party – they'll be dead nuts on it. And Evelyn Bray plays dance music like a professional.

AGATHA: What a lovely joke. I say – let's make it a fancy-dress affair while we're about it.

SYBIL: Oh, let's have fireworks on the lawn and Salomé dances* and a looping-the-loop performance.

AGATHA: That's talking nonsense. But fancy dress is so easily managed. I went to a ball in North Devon three years ago as Summer, and it was all done at a moment's notice. Just a dress of some soft creamy material with roses in my hair and a few sprays of flowers round the skirt. I've got the dress with me somewhere, and it wouldn't need very much alteration.

SYBIL: It will only want letting out a bit at the waist, and you can call yourself St Martin's Summer.*

AGATHA: How dare you say such things! Really, you're the most spiteful-tongued person I know. I should think you'd better go as an East Wind.*

SYBIL: My dear Agatha, I'm not one of the Babes in the Wood, so I wish you'd stop covering me with leaves.* And don't let us start quarrelling. Of course you're as jumpy as a grasshopper at the idea of this dance, and I suppose you flatter yourself that you're going to pull it off with Trevor. Because a man has refused you twice there's no particular reason for supposing that he'll accept you at the third bidding. It's merely a superstition.

AGATHA (furiously): You utterly odious fable-monger! I suppose it's considered clever to say ill-natured, untrue things about people you happen to be jealous of.

MRS VULPY: My dear girls, don't waste time in a sparring match. There's no sense quarrelling when we want to get our little scheme started.

SYBIL: I don't want to quarrel; I'm only too ready to be accommodating all round. If I do chance to land a certain eligible individual in my net I'm quite willing to turn my second-best prospect over to anyone that applies for him; quite a darling, with a decent rent roll, and a perfect martyr to asthma; ever so many climates that he can't live in, and you'll have to keep him on a gravel soil. Awfully good arrangement. A husband with asthma has all the advantages of a captive golf ball; you always know pretty well where to put your hand on him when you want him.

AGATHA: But if I had a really nice man for a husband I should want him to be able to come with me wherever I went.

SYBIL: A woman who takes her husband about with her everywhere is like a cat that goes on playing with a mouse long after she's killed it.

MRS VULPY: First catch your mouse. Which brings us back to the subject of the dance. I think we agree that fancy dress is out of the question?

CLARE: There wouldn't be time.

MRS VULPY: Well, why not make it a sheet-and-pillowcase dance?

(*They all stare at her.*)

Quite simple: everyone drapes themselves in sheets, with a folded pillowcase arranged as a headdress, and a little linen mask completes the domino effect. No trouble, only takes ten minutes to arrange, and at a given time everyone sheds their masks and headgear, and the sheets make a most effective sort of Greek costume. Lulu Duchess of Dulverton* gave quite a smart sheet-and-pillowcase at Bovery the other day.

AGATHA: Was it respectable?

MRS VULPY: Absolutely. Oh, do take your blessed bramble bush somewhere else.

(AGATHA, *who has impaled* MRS VULPY*'s skirt on a trail of briars, makes violent efforts to disentangle her.*)

No, please leave my skirt where it is. I only want the brambles removed.

AGATHA: That's the worst of briars — they do catch on to one's clothes so.

MRS VULPY: That is one of the reasons why I never sit down in a bramble patch for choice. Of course, if one has a tame hedge following one about the house, one can't help it.

AGATHA (*gathering up remains of her foliage*): Well, I shall go and do the dining-room vases now and leave you irritable things to work out the dance programme. I'll think out a list of people we can invite. (*Exit, door left front.*)

CLARE: Agatha would be almost tolerable in the Arctic regions where the vegetation is too restricted to be used as house decoration.

SYBIL: Look here, I'll bike over to the Abingdons' and get things in marching order there. I've just time before lunch. You're going to help us, I suppose, Clare?

CLARE: Oh, if you are all bent on having a domestic earthquake, I'll stand in with you. I'll send notes over to Evelyn and the Drummond boys. But I know the whole thing will be a horrid fizzle.

SYBIL: You dear old thing. You always turn up trumps when it comes to the pinch.

CLARE: If you dare to call me a dear old thing I'll allude to you in public as a brave little woman. So there.

MRS VULPY: Well, if you two are going to start sparring, I shall go and write letters. (*Exit, door right back.*)

CLARE: There's something I don't like about that woman. She looks at me sometimes in a way that's almost malicious. What on earth did Agatha bring her down here for?

SYBIL: Mrs Vulpy is somewhat of a rough diamond, no doubt.

CLARE: So many people who are described as rough diamonds turn out to be merely rough paste.

SYBIL: Even paste has its uses.

CLARE: Oh, afflictions of most kinds have their uses, I suppose, but one needn't go out of one's way to import them.

(*Exit* SYBIL, *right back; enter* TREVOR, *left back; he is about to sit on couch.*)

Be careful where you sit, Trevor. Agatha has been shedding bits of bramble all over the room.

(*They both begin picking bits of leaf, etc., off the couch.*)

When that parable was being read at prayers this morning about going to the hedges and byways to fetch in the halt and the blind,* I couldn't help thinking Agatha wouldn't have stopped at that: she'd have brought in the hedges as well.

TREVOR (*seating himself with caution on couch*): I've just had about a wheelbarrow-load of gorse prickles removed from the cozy corner in the smoking room.

CLARE: Gorse prickles? (*Seats herself on couch.*)

TREVOR: Agatha said it was a Japanese design. If it had been an accident I could have forgiven it. I say, Clare, do you know you have got rather beautiful eyes?

CLARE: How should I know? You've never mentioned it before.

TREVOR: Oh, well, I noticed it long ago, but it takes me ages to put my thoughts into words.

CLARE: That's rather unfortunate where compliments are concerned. By the time it occurs to you to tell me that I've got a nice profile I shall probably have developed a double chin.

TREVOR: And that will be the time when you'll be best pleased at being told you've got a nice profile. So you see, there's some sense in holding back a compliment.

CLARE: Well, don't be horrid and sensible just when you were beginning to be interesting. It's not often one catches you in the mood for paying compliments. Please begin over again.

TREVOR: Item, a pair of beautiful eyes, one rather nice chin, with power to add to its number. Quite a lot of very pretty hair, standing in its own grounds – or is it semi-detached?

CLARE: I don't think your compliments are a bit nice; I don't mind how long you keep them back.

TREVOR: I haven't finished yet. (*Takes her hand.*) Do you know, Clare, you've got the most charming hand in the world, because it's a friendly hand. I think if you were once friends with a fellow you'd always be friends with him, even—

CLARE: Even...?

TREVOR: Even if you married him, and that's saying a great deal.

CLARE: I think if I liked a man well enough to marry him I should always be the best of friends with him.

71

(*Enter* LUDOVIC; *bustles over to escritoire.*)

LUDOVIC (*as they let go each other's hands*): Hullo, has Trevor
  been telling you your fortune?
CLARE (*rising*): Nothing so romantic; he's been explaining
  the fingerprint system of criminal investigation. If I ever
  strangle Agatha in a moment of justifiable irritation
  Trevor will be a most damaging witness.

(LUDOVIC *rings bell and then seats himself at escritoire.*)

TREVOR: Shall I be disturbing you if I smoke a cigarette here?
LUDOVIC: Not in the least. I like seeing people idle when I'm
  occupied. It gives me the impression that I'm working so
  much harder than I am.
CLARE: Don't be long over your cigarette, Trevor, you've got
  to be let into a conspiracy that Mr Ludovic isn't supposed
  to know anything about. (*Exit.*)
TREVOR: Are they plotting to give you a birthday present or
  something of that sort?
LUDOVIC: Nothing so laudable.

(*Enter* WILLIAM, *right front.*)

WILLIAM: Did you ring, sir?
LUDOVIC: Yes, just arrange the flowers.
WILLIAM: Yes, sir. (*Gathers up flowers and foliage from various
  places where* AGATHA *has stacked and strewn them and
  proceeds to rearrange them with considerable taste.*)
LUDOVIC (*to* TREVOR): No, it's your despotic mother who
  mustn't get wind of the plot. I am merely the innocent
  bystander.

TREVOR: I'm awfully fond of my mother, of course, but I must admit things would be a little more comfortable if she wasn't quite so... so...

LUDOVIC: Exactly. But she always has been, and she always will be. As regards household affairs, of course, I've no right to express an opinion, but her constant supervision of the political affairs of the neighbourhood is extremely embarrassing to the party. My prospective candidature down here is becoming more and more doubtful under the circumstances. Hortensia is not content with having her finger in the pie; she wants to put the whole dish into her pocket.

WILLIAM (*who is standing near doorway*): Mrs Bavvel is crossing the hall, sir.

LUDOVIC (*becomes violently busy at escritoire*): The factory system in East Prussia presents many interesting points of comparison...

(*Enter* HORTENSIA, *right.* LUDOVIC *rises.*)

Ah, Hortensia.

HORTENSIA: William, what are you doing here?

WILLIAM: Arranging the flowers, ma'am.

HORTENSIA: They don't want arranging every day. They were arranged only yesterday.

(HORTENSIA *seats herself on chair in centre of stage.* LUDOVIC *resumes seat.*)

WILLIAM: It was brought on prematurely, ma'am.

LUDOVIC: Agatha had been trying some new effects in autumnal foliage; I told William to put things straight a bit.

HORTENSIA: I see. And where is Adolphus?

WILLIAM: The cockatoo, ma'am? She's drying in the pantry after her bath.

HORTENSIA: It's not his day for a bath. He always bathes on Thursday.

WILLIAM: She seemed restless, as if she wanted it, ma'am.

HORTENSIA: In future, remember he bathes on Thursdays only. And William?

WILLIAM: Yes, ma'am?

HORTENSIA: I think I've spoken about it before. You always hear me allude to the cockatoo as he, or Adolphus; therefore you are not to speak of him in the feminine gender.

WILLIAM: Yes, ma'am. (*Exit, left front.*)

HORTENSIA: A quiet-mannered boy, and always behaves reverently at prayers, but I'm afraid he's inclined to be opinionated. What coverts* are you shooting this afternoon, Trevor?

TREVOR: The other side of the long plantation.

HORTENSIA: I understand that you are employing one of the Brady boys as a beater. I do not approve of the selection. Kindly discontinue his services.

TREVOR: But Mother, the Bradys are dreadfully poor.

HORTENSIA: Not deservingly poor.* Mrs Brady is the most thriftless woman in the parish. Some people can't help being poor, but Mrs Brady is poor as if she enjoyed it. I'm not going to have that sort of thing encouraged.

LUDOVIC (*rising from seat*): There is another aspect of the matter which I think you are losing sight of, Hortensia. Mrs Brady may be poor in this world's goods, but she is rich in relatives. She has a husband and one or two uncles, and at least three brothers, and they all have votes. The non-employment of the Brady boy may lose us all those votes at the next election.

HORTENSIA: My dear Ludovic, I am not inattentive to local political needs. I supervise the issue of pamphlets dealing with the questions of the day to all electors, in monthly instalments. When the next election comes you may be sure it won't take me by surprise.

LUDOVIC: No, but the result may. (*Resumes his seat.*)

HORTENSIA: Trevor, oblige me by taking an amended list of beaters to the head keeper, with the Brady boy left out. Go now, or you will forget.

TREVOR (*rising unwillingly*): As you will, Mother. He made a very good beater, you know.

HORTENSIA: But not a suitable one.

(*Exit* TREVOR. LUDOVIC *throws up his hands.*)

Who is this Mrs Vulpy that Agatha has brought down? I don't care for the look of her.

LUDOVIC: I believe Agatha met her at Folkestone.

HORTENSIA: That doesn't make it any better. Agatha says she's seen trouble, but she doesn't explain what sort of trouble. Some women see trouble with their eyes open.

LUDOVIC: I believe she has a husband in Johannesburg.

HORTENSIA: To have a husband in Johannesburg might be a source of anxiety or inconvenience, but it can hardly be called seeing trouble.

LUDOVIC: Agatha is so good-natured that she's very easily imposed on.

HORTENSIA: I wish her good nature would occasionally take the form of consulting other people's interests. I suppose this Mrs Vulpy is married after a fashion, though we really know nothing about her. She may be merely a husband-hunting adventuress, and of course Trevor is sufficiently important as a matrimonial prize to attract that sort of woman. Agatha ought to be more careful.

LUDOVIC: Wouldn't it be as well, in view of such dangers, if Trevor were to bestir himself to find a suitable wife?

HORTENSIA: Nothing of the sort. I must ask you not to give him any advice of that sort. Trevor is far younger than his years, and there is no need to suggest marriage to him for a long while to come. If I thought he had any present intentions that way I should be far more particular what sort of girls I had staying down here. Sybil Bomont and Miss Henessey, for instance: I've no objections to them as guests, but I should require quite a different type of young woman for a daughter-in-law.

LUDOVIC: Trevor may have his own views on the subject.

HORTENSIA: Hitherto he has expressed none. I must go and write to the Bishop.

LUDOVIC: About Trevor?

HORTENSIA (*rising*): *No*. About the Dean of Minehead.

LUDOVIC: What has the Dean been doing?

HORTENSIA: He has treated me with flippancy. I had written asking if he could give me any material for a lecture I am going to give next week on the Puritan movement in England. He replies on a postcard. (*Reads:*) 'The Puritan movement was a disease, wholesome though irritating, which was only malignant if its after-effects were not guarded against.' Things have come to a disgraceful pass when a Church dignitary can treat the Puritan movement in that spirit.

LUDOVIC: Perhaps the Dean was only exercising a little clerical humour.

HORTENSIA: I don't think the subject lends itself to jest, and I certainly don't intend that my lecture shall be regarded in a spirit of frivolity. I've something better to do than provide an outlet for Deanery humour. My letter to the Bishop will contain some pretty plain speaking.

LUDOVIC: My dear Hortensia, the Dean of Minehead is one of the few churchmen in these parts who give us political support. It would be rather unfortunate to fall out with him.

HORTENSIA: In my opinion, it would be still more unfortunate to tolerate postcard flippancies on serious subjects from men in his position. I shall ask the Bishop, among other things, whether it is not high time that certain clerical clowns ceased their unfair competition with the music halls.

(*Exit* HORTENSIA, *right back.* LUDOVIC *goes through pantomime of tragic disgust. Enter* BUTLER, *left back.*)

BUTLER: Mr St Gall to see you, sir.

LUDOVIC: René! What on earth brings him down here? Show him in.

(*Exit* BUTLER, *left back. Enter* RENÉ, *left back; crosses stage without shaking hands, looks at himself in mirror, right.*)

RENÉ: I've lost my mother.

LUDOVIC (*wheeling round in chair*): Do I understand you to mean that your mother is dead?

RENÉ (*who has carefully settled himself in armchair, right*): Oh, nothing so hackneyed. I don't think my mother will ever die as long as she can get credit. She was a Whortleford, you know, and the Whortlefords never waste anything. No, she's simply disappeared, and I was wired for. It was most inconvenient.

LUDOVIC: But can't she be found?

RENÉ: The butler says she can't. Personally I haven't tried. Only got down late last night. And I've had to come away with simply nothing to wear. I've been in town for the last three days having some clothes made, and I was to have had two new lounge suits tried on this morning for the first time. Naturally I'm a bit upset.

LUDOVIC: But about your mother's disappearance – aren't you doing anything?

RENÉ: Oh, everything that could be done at short notice. We've notified the police and the family solicitors and consulted a crystal-gazer, and we've told the dairy to send half a pint less milk every day till further notice. I can't think of anything else to do. It's the first time I've lost a mother, you know.

LUDOVIC: But do you mean to say there's absolutely no trace of her? Why, I saw her in church only last Sunday.

RENÉ: I expect they've looked for her there; the butler says they've searched everywhere. The servants have been awfully kind and helpful about it. They say they must put their trust in Christian Science, and go on drawing their wages as if nothing had happened. That's all very well, but no amount of Christian Science will help me to be fitted on when I'm here and my clothes are in Sackville Street, will it?

LUDOVIC: I think you might show a little natural anxiety and emotion.

RENÉ: But I am showing emotion in a hundred little ways, if you'd only notice them. To begin with, I'm walking about practically naked. This suit I've got on was paid for last month, so you may judge how old it is. And that reminds me – I wish you'd do something for me. Something awfully kind and pet-lamb in my hour of trouble. Lend me that emerald scarf pin that you hardly ever wear. It would go so well with this tie, and I should forget how shabbily I'm dressed.

LUDOVIC: It would go so well that it would forget to find its way back again. Things that are lent to you, René, are like a hopeless passion: they're never returned. In the light of past experience I absolutely refuse to lend you a thirty-guinea scarf pin.

RENÉ: How true it is that when one weeps one weeps alone. Anyway, you might lend me your pearl and turquoise one; the pearl is a very poor one, and it can't be worth anything like thirty guineas.

LUDOVIC: I don't see why I should be expected to make you a present of it, even if it only cost five.

RENÉ: Oh, well, after all, I've lost a mother. I make less fuss about that than you do at the prospect of separation from a five-guinea scarf pin. You might show a little kindness to a poor grass orphan.* And, Ludovic, now that you've practically given way on that matter, I want you to turn your attention to something that's been worrying me dreadfully of late.

LUDOVIC: Gracious, what have you been doing now?

RENÉ: Oh, it isn't now – the mischief was done twenty-three years ago, and then it wasn't exactly my doing. It's just this: that I'm twenty-three years old. If my mother had only held me over a matter of four years I should be nineteen now, which is the only age worth being. Women always rush things so. I shouldn't mind so much being twenty-three if I had the money to carry it off well. The mater* does the best she can for me; she can't afford me an allowance, but she borrows money whenever she can from friends and acquaintances, and sends me haphazard cheques. It's quite exciting getting a letter from home. Of course, that sort of thing can't go on indefinitely, and now that my only source of income has disappeared without leaving a postal address things have nearly come to a crisis. One can't treat life indefinitely as a prolonged Saturday-to-Monday. There are always the Tuesdays to be reckoned with.

LUDOVIC: I don't like to suggest anything so unbecoming as an occupation, but can't you manage to get entangled with a salary of some sort?

RENÉ: It's not so beastly easy. I've tried designing posters, and for three weeks I was assistant editor of a paper devoted to fancy mice. The devotion was all on one side. Now, Ludovic, if you'd only do what you sometimes half-promised to do, and make me your personal private secretary, and let me do Parliamentary correspondence for you, and tell female deputations that they can't see you because you're in your bath, and all that sort of thing that a busy man can't do for himself—

LUDOVIC: My dear boy, I'm not at the present moment a Member of Parliament; I'm not even standing as a candidate.

RENÉ: But, Ludo, why aren't you? You know you've had a hankering that way for a long time, and you can easily afford it. And it isn't a difficult job. All one has to do is to boil with indignation at discreet intervals over something – the Jews in Russia or impurity in beer or lawlessness in the

Church of England. It doesn't matter particularly what, as long as you really boil. The public likes a touch of the samovar* about its representatives. And, then, if you want to be a Parliamentary wit, *that* isn't difficult nowadays. If the Government is making a mess of Persian affairs just mew like a Persian kitten whenever a minister gets up to speak. It isn't anything really hard I'm asking of you.

LUDOVIC: Thanks very much for coaching me. But an indispensable preliminary to all this brilliance is that I should be elected.

RENÉ: You could easily get a seat down here if you wanted to. They've always wanted one of the Bavvels to stand, and old Spindleham is not likely to last another session, so the ball is practically at your feet.

LUDOVIC: My dear René, under present circumstances Briony would be an impossible headquarters from which to conduct an election campaign. Have you considered that Hortensia would have her finger in the pie all the time? She would speak at my meetings and pledge me to the most appalling social and political doctrines. She would get down the most unfortunate specimens of the party to support me – in fact, by the time election day came round I should feel inclined to vote against myself. I should very probably be defeated, and if I got in Hortensia would look on me as her nominee, sent to Westminster to represent her views on every subject under the sun. I shouldn't have half an hour's peace. No, as long as Hortensia remains in the foreground I shan't contest a seat in this part of the country. That's absolutely certain.

RENÉ: Ludovic, this Hortensia business is getting to be absurd. Everything you want to do down here you run up against Hortensia, Mrs Bavvel. When *are* you going to get Trevor married and the old woman dethroned?

LUDOVIC: My dear René, as if we hadn't tried! Talk about bringing a horse to the water – we've brought water to the horse, gallons of it, and put it right under his nose. We've advertised eligible young women as if they had been breakfast foods.

RENÉ: And here am I, twenty-three years old, expecting to wait indefinitely for my secretaryship and my daily bread until Trevor chooses to suit himself with a wife. It's really ridiculous. That's the worst of you middle-aged folks, if I may say so without offence. You're so jolly well content to wait for things to happen. It's only the old and the quite young who really know the value of hurry.

LUDOVIC: But, bless my soul, we can't compel Trevor to marry.

RENÉ: It's absurd of him to persist in celibacy that he isn't qualified for. He's decent enough in his way, but he hasn't got the strength of character to fit him for the graver responsibilities of bachelorhood. Can't he be rushed into marrying somebody?

LUDOVIC: Rushing Trevor is not exactly a hopeful operation. It's rather suggestive of stampeding a tortoise; at the same time, I may tell you in confidence that something desperate of that nature is going to be tried tomorrow night in the absence of Hortensia and myself at Panfold.

RENÉ: Oh, Ludovic! What?

LUDOVIC: You must ask Sybil or some of the others for details. I know nothing about it and entirely disapprove, but the idea originated with me. Hush!

(*Enter* HORTENSIA, *door right back.* LUDOVIC *and* RENÉ *rise to their feet.*)

HORTENSIA: I want you to read my letter to the Bishop. Oh, Mr St Gall, I didn't know the neighbourhood was honoured with your presence. I needn't ask if you're on a holiday – that is a permanent condition with you, I believe.

LUDOVIC: Mr St Gall has lost his mother – she's disappeared.

HORTENSIA: Disappeared! What an extraordinary thing to do. Had she any reasons for disappearing?

RENÉ: Oh, several, but my mother would never do anything for a reason.

HORTENSIA: But was anything troubling her? (*Sits, chair centre of stage.*)

RENÉ: Oh, nothing of that kind. She's one of those people with a conscience silk-lined throughout.

LUDOVIC: Has she any relatives that she might have gone to?

RENÉ: Relatives? None that she's on speaking terms with. She was a Whortleford, you know, and the Whortlefords don't speak. There is a cousin of hers, a Canon, somewhere in the Midlands; he's got peculiar views – he believes in a future life, or else he doesn't, I forget which. The mater and he used to be rather chummy, but a hen came in between them.*

HORTENSIA: A hen?

RENÉ: Yes, a bronze Orpington or some such exotic breed; the mater sold it to him at a rather exotic price. It turned out afterwards that the bird was an abstainer from the egg habit, and the Canon wanted his money back. I read some of the letters that passed between them. I don't think the mater is likely to have gone *there*.

HORTENSIA: But there is an alarming side to this disappearance which you don't seem to appreciate. Something dreadful may have happened.

RENÉ: It has. I had been measured for two lounge suits, one of them in a rather taking shade of copper beech, and they were to have been tried on for the first time this morning—

LUDOVIC (*hurriedly*): As everything is naturally rather at sixes and sevens at the Oaks, I have asked St Gall to stay to lunch. I suppose we can give him a bite of something?

HORTENSIA (*coldly*): I am always glad to show hospitality to your friends, Ludovic. I'll read you my letter to the Bishop at a more convenient moment. I'm just going to see Laura Gubbings; she's going out to Afghanistan as a missionary, you know. That country has been scandalously neglected in the way of missionary effort.

LUDOVIC: There are considerable political and geographical difficulties in the way.

HORTENSIA: Not insuperable, however.

LUDOVIC: Perhaps not, but extremely likely to expand. We usually set out on these affairs with the intention of devoting a certain amount of patient effort in making the natives reasonably glad at the introduction of mission work; then we find ourselves involved in a much bigger effort to make them reasonably sorry for having killed the missionaries.

HORTENSIA: Really, Ludovic, your reasoning is preposterous. I should be the first to oppose anything in the shape of armed aggression in Central Asia.

LUDOVIC: If you would oppose Miss Gubbings' missionary designs on that region I should feel more comfortable.

RENÉ: I say, can't she take me with her?

HORTENSIA: I don't really see in what capacity you could be included in a mission party.

RENÉ: I could give my famous imitation of a nautch girl.* That would fetch the Afghans in shoals, and then Miss Gubbings could hold overflow meetings and convert them.

HORTENSIA: A nautch girl?

RENÉ: Yes, I did it for some friends at St Petersburg and they just loved it. They said I got as far East as anyone could be expected to go. If I wasn't suffering under a domestic bereavement I'd do it for you now.

HORTENSIA: Not at Briony, thank you! St Petersburg may applaud such performances if it pleases. From the things I've heard from there—

RENÉ: Oh, for the matter of that, the things one hears about the Afghans – there is a proverb in that country—

LUDOVIC (hurriedly): In any case, Miss Gubbings is hardly likely to accept your collaboration in her labours.

HORTENSIA: Miss Gubbings is going out with a religious mission, not with a café chantant.* From your description of your performance and from what I can guess of its nature, I don't think it would be likely to enhance either our moral or national reputation in the eyes of the emir's subjects. (Rises from chair.) A boy masquerading as a nautch girl! (Exit, door left front.)

RENÉ: Another avenue of employment closed to me. By the way, where is Trevor? I want to ask him to lend me some sleeve links. These ones won't go at all with the scarf pin you're lending me.

LUDOVIC: You'll probably find him at the head keeper's lodge. Lunch is at one sharp.

(*Exit* RENÉ, *door left back.*)

Now perhaps I can have a few moments to myself and the Prussian Factory Acts.

(*Enter* SPARROWBY, *right back.*)

SPARROWBY (*seating himself astride of chair, centre*): I say, I wish you'd do something to help me.

LUDOVIC (*looks over shoulder and then back to pamphlet*): If it's anything in the way of sleeve links or scarf pins you're too late.

SPARROWBY: Oh, nothing of that sort—

LUDOVIC: Or are you looking for a strayed relative? I can get you the address of a crystal-gazer.

SPARROWBY: Oh, no, I haven't lost anyone; quite the reverse, dear old chap, I've *found* her.

LUDOVIC (*half turning round*): Not Mrs St Gall?

SPARROWBY: Mrs St Gall? Dear, no! I've found the one woman I could ever want to make my wife, and I want you to help me to pull it off.

LUDOVIC (*returning to the perusal of his pamphlet*): Oh, I see. Delighted to be of any use to you. I don't quite know how you pull these things off, and I'm rather occupied these days, but on Wednesday next, in the early part of the afternoon, I can spare you an hour or two. (*Cuts page of pamphlet and continues reading.*)

SPARROWBY: Oh, but one can't fix a precise time for that sort of thing. The trouble I'm in is that she won't be serious about it. She—

LUDOVIC: What does '*Bewegungslosigkeit*' mean in English?*

SPARROWBY: Oh, I don't know – it's a German word, isn't it? I don't know any German.

(LUDOVIC *consults dictionary.*)

She treats it as a sort of temporary infatuation on my part. She won't realise how hopelessly I'm in love with her.

LUDOVIC (*yawning*): I thought it was the hopelessness of your suit that she did realise. Who is the lady?

SPARROWBY: Sybil Bomont.

LUDOVIC (*leaping round in his seat and letting dictionary fall*): Impossible! Out of the question. You mustn't think of marrying Sybil Bomont.

SPARROWBY: But I can think of nothing else. Why mustn't I marry her?

LUDOVIC: You must dismiss the matter completely from your mind. Go fishing in Norway or fall in love with a chorus girl. There are heaps of chorus girls who are willing to marry commoners if you set the right way about it. But you mustn't think of Sybil Bomont.

SPARROWBY: But what is the objection? Surely there's no madness in her family?

LUDOVIC (*contemplatively*): Madness? No. Oh, no. At least, not that one knows of. Certainly her father lives at West Kensington, but he is sane on most other subjects.

SPARROWBY: Then what is this mysterious obstacle? There is nothing against me, I suppose? I am fairly well off, as far as income is concerned.

LUDOVIC: Ah! And to what sort of environment are you proposing to take this young girl, who has been carefully brought up and kept shielded from the coarser realities of life?

SPARROWBY: Well, I live very quietly in the country and farm a few acres of my own.

LUDOVIC: Precisely: I had heard stories to that effect. Now, my dear Sparrowby, the moral atmosphere of a farm, however amateur and non-paying the farm may be, is most unsuitable for a young woman who has been brought up in the seclusion of a town life. Farming involves cows, and I consider that cows carry the maternal instinct to indelicate excess. They seem to regard the universe in general as an imperfectly weaned calf. And then poultry – you must admit that the private life of the domestic barn-door fowl – well, there's remarkably little privacy about it.

SPARROWBY: But, my dear Bavvel—

LUDOVIC: And are you quite sure that you are free to pay court to Miss Bomont – that you have no other entanglements?

SPARROWBY: Entanglements? Why, certainly not.

LUDOVIC: Think a moment. What about Miss Clifford?

SPARROWBY: Agatha Clifford? You must be dreaming! I haven't the ghost of an entanglement with her.

LUDOVIC: I thought I saw you both on rather intimate terms at breakfast this morning.

SPARROWBY (*indignantly*): She upset a sardine on to my knees.

LUDOVIC: I suppose you encouraged her to.

SPARROWBY: Encouraged her? Why, it ruined a pair of flannel trousers!

LUDOVIC: Well, I expect her sardine was just as irrevocably damaged. Anyway, you condoned her action – I heard you tell her that it didn't matter.

SPARROWBY: Oh, I had to say that. What else could one say?

LUDOVIC: If anyone upset a sardine on to my lap I should find no difficulty in keeping the conversation from flagging. The difficulty would be to avoid saying too much. In your case I think you were rather too eloquently silent. The spilling of a sardine on to your lap may seem a small thing to you, but you must remember that women attach more importance to these trifles than we do. Believe me, I have watched your perhaps unconscious attentions to Miss Clifford with interest, and if anything I can do—

SPARROWBY: But I assure you—

(*Enter* AGATHA *and* SYBIL, *door left back.*)

AGATHA: Everything's going splendidly. Everyone whom we've asked is coming, and Cook has been given a dark hint to have some fruit salads and mayonnaise and that sort of thing accidentally on hand— (*To* LUDOVIC:) Oh, I forgot you weren't to know anything about it. Promise that you'll forget that you heard anything.

LUDOVIC: I assure you I heard nothing. I was struggling with some technicalities in a German pamphlet. Dear Miss Bomont, do show me where I can find a better dictionary than this one.

SYBIL: Come along. There's one somewhere in the library.

LUDOVIC: And, Agatha, Mr Sparrowby wants you to help him to dig up some ferns for a rockery he's making at home.

(LUDOVIC *holds door, left front, open for* SYBIL; *exeunt.*)

SPARROWBY: I say—

AGATHA (*cheerfully*): By all means; let's come now. I love rooting up ferns. Here are some baskets. (*Fishes three large garden baskets out of chest.*)

SPARROWBY: But it's nearly lunchtime, and I don't really—

AGATHA: Never mind lunch. There's sure to be something cold that we can peck at if we're late. Come on; the trowels are out in the toolshed. I know a lovely damp wood where we can grub about for hours.

SPARROWBY: But I've got rheumatism.

AGATHA: So have I. Come on.

(*Gives him two baskets to carry and leads the way off by door, right back.*)

ACT II

The hall, Briony Manor.

CLARE *and* TREVOR *seated on couch, centre of stage. Enter*
AGATHA, *door left; passes behind them. All three dressed in sheet*
costume, with hood thrown back, no masks.

AGATHA: I say, Trevor, it's going splendidly! (*Exit, door right*
back.)

CLARE: If you ask me, it's going as flat as can be. No one
seems to want to dance, and Cook is scared to death
and has only sent us up half the amount of supper that
we asked for.

TREVOR: There's enough to drink, anyhow; I saw to that.
I went down to the cellar myself.

CLARE: Yes, and the result will be that just when we want to
be hurrying everyone off the premises they'll be getting
festive and reckless, and your august and awful mother
will run up against half of them on the doorstep, or
meet them in the drive.

(*Enter at door right back veiled figure, who glides up to them.*)

Hallo, who's this?

(SYBIL *unmasks and throws back hood.*)

Oh, Sybil, I might have guessed.

SYBIL (*seating herself, armchair centre of stage*): I fled away from that tiresome Sparrowby person who keeps on pestering me to sit out with him. Clare, dear, do go and relieve Evelyn – she's played about six dances running.

CLARE: Oh, Evelyn would play all night without feeling tired. (*Rises.*) But one excuse is as good as another, I suppose. (*Walks towards door, right.*)

SYBIL: I don't know what you mean.

(*Exit* CLARE, *door right back.*)

It's going awfully flat.

TREVOR (*lighting cigarette*): Oh, a frightful fizzle. I think everyone is a bit scared at what they're doing.

SYBIL: I know I am. There'll be fine fireworks tomorrow when Her Majesty gets to hear of it.

TREVOR: Fireworks! There'll be a full-sized earthquake. I think I shall go cub-hunting if there's a meet within reasonable distance.

SYBIL: You won't find many of us here when you return. We shall be cleared out in a batch, like Chinese coolies. Trevor, why on earth don't you marry and get rid of this one-woman rule at Briony? With all due respect, your mother is no joke. She's perfectly awful.

TREVOR: Oh, I suppose I shall marry somebody some day, but it's the choosing business that is so beastly complicated. Think of the millions and millions of nice women there are in the world, and then of the fact that one can only marry one of them – it makes marrying an awfully ticklish matter. It's like choosing which puppies you're going to keep out of a large litter; you can never be sure that you haven't drowned the wrong ones.

SYBIL: Oh, but if you go on those lines you'll never marry anyone. You should just have a look round at the girls you personally know and like and make your choice from one of them. You'd soon find out whether she responded or not. I believe in grasping one's nettle.

TREVOR: But supposing there are half a dozen nettles and you don't know which to grasp?

SYBIL: Oh, come, we're getting on. Half a dozen is better than millions and millions. And there must always be someone whom you prefer out of the half-dozen. There's Agatha, for instance. Of course, she is your cousin, but that doesn't really matter. And in her way she's not a bad sort.

TREVOR: She passed through the hall just before you came in. If I'm to ask her to marry me I'd better go and do it now before I forget it.

SYBIL (*alarmed*): Oh, don't go and propose to her just because I suggested it. You'd make me feel an awful matchmaker, and I should never forgive myself if it turned out wrong. Besides, I doubt very much if she'd make the sort of mistress you'd want for Briony. One has to think of so many things, hasn't one?

TREVOR: Precisely my standpoint. And if Agatha turned out a disappointment I couldn't give her away to the gardener's boy, like an unsatisfactory puppy. You see, it isn't so easy to grasp the nettle when you really come to do it.

SYBIL: Oh, well, Agatha doesn't exhaust the list. There's Clare, for instance – she's got some good points, don't you think?

TREVOR: You don't say so with much conviction.

SYBIL: I'm awfully good pals with Clare, but that doesn't prevent me from recognising that she's got rather a queer temper at times; the things that she says sometimes are simply hateful, and she's not a bit straightforward. I could tell you of little things she's done—

(*Enter from door centre veiled figure.*)

Who on earth is this?

(SPARROWBY *throws off hood and mask and seats himself on small chair facing* SYBIL.)

SPARROWBY: I've been following all sorts of figures about, thinking they were you. But I knew all the time they couldn't be you, because I didn't feel a thrill when I was near them. I always feel a thrill when I'm near you.

SYBIL (*viciously*): I wish you never felt thrills, then.

SPARROWBY: You're dreadfully unkind, Sybil, but I know you don't mean what you say.

SYBIL: Sorry you find my conversation meaningless.

SPARROWBY: Oh, I didn't mean that!

SYBIL: We seem equally unfortunate in our meanings.

SPARROWBY: I say, Sybil, I wish you'd take me a little more seriously.

94

SYBIL: One would think you were an attack of measles.

(*Enter* MRS VULPY *with* DRUMMOND, *door left, both unhooded. She catches sight of trio and rushes up.*)

MRS VULPY (*to* DRUMMOND): Excuse me one moment. (*To* SPARROWBY:) Naughty man, you know you promised me the kitchen lancers.* Come along. Hurry.

SPARROWBY (*rising unwillingly*): But they're playing a waltz now.

MRS VULPY: They're getting ready for the lancers. Come on.

(*Exeunt* MRS VULPY, SPARROWBY *and* DRUMMOND, *door right back.*

SYBIL: The Vulpy woman is rather a brick at times. I say – *Trevor!*

(*During* SPARROWBY *duologue* TREVOR *has fallen asleep. Wakes hurriedly.*)

TREVOR: I nearly went off to sleep. Please excuse my manners. I was up awfully early this morning.

SYBIL: Well, do keep awake now. We're in the middle of a most interesting conversation.

TREVOR: Let's see – you were recommending me to marry Clare Henessey.

SYBIL: Oh, well – I don't think I went as far as that. Clare and I are first-rate pals, and I should awfully like to see her make a good marriage, but I'd be rather sorry for her husband, all the same. If anything rubs her the wrong way her temper goes queer at once, like milk in thunder-time, and she simply says the most ill-natured things.

TREVOR: That's another ungraspable nettle, then. I told you it wasn't so jolly easy.

SYBIL: But, Trevor, there are surely others, only you're too lazy to think of them.

TREVOR: As to thinking of them, I am not too lazy to do that; it's the further stages I'm deficient in.

SYBIL: Of course I sympathise with your difficulty. I wish I could find you someone really nice, someone who would enter into all your pursuits and share your ambitions and be a genuine companion to you.

TREVOR: I hate that sort.

SYBIL: Do you? How funny. At least – I don't know – I rather think I agree with you. Some women make dreadful nuisances of themselves that way. Well, you don't give me much help in choosing you a wife.

TREVOR: What do you think of Mrs Vulpy?

SYBIL: What! That woman with nasturtium-coloured hair and barmaid manners? Surely you're not attracted by her?

TREVOR: I didn't say I was. I asked you what you thought of her.

SYBIL: Oh, as to that, not a bad sort in her way, I suppose. Some people call her a rough diamond. If it was my declaration I should call her a defensive spade. But anyhow, she's married, so she doesn't come into our discussion.

TREVOR: I want to tell you something – something that concerns you alone.

SYBIL: What is it?

TREVOR: Your hair's coming down behind.

SYBIL: Oh, bother! It's that horrid hood arrangement. I'll
fly upstairs and put it right. (*Rises.*) I say, Trev, there's a
much nicer sitting-out place on the landing, near that
old carved press, where the tiresome Sparrowby person
won't find me. Come up in two minutes' time – there's
a dear.

TREVOR: Right-oh!

SYBIL: Now, don't go to sleep.

(*Exit* SYBIL, *up staircase left. Enter* AGATHA, *door right back;
passes along back of stage.*)

AGATHA: Everything's going swimmingly; it's a huge success.

(*Exit* AGATHA, *door left back. Enter* RENÉ, *door centre, in evening dress with smoking jacket, carrying bottle of wine, wine glass,
some grapes and peaches. Seats himself on armchair near small
table.*)

RENÉ: Going rather flat, isn't it?

TREVOR: Frightful fizzle. I'm so sleepy myself that I can only
just keep my eyes open. Was up at the farm awfully early
this morning.

RENÉ: Some shorthorn or bantam was going to have young
ones, I suppose? In the country animals are always having young ones; passes the time away, I suppose. I know
a lady in Warwickshire who runs a rabbit farm. She has
musical boxes set up over the hutches.

TREVOR: Musical boxes?

RENÉ: Yes, they play the wedding march from *Lohengrin* at decent intervals. I'm going to ask you an extremely personal question.

TREVOR: If it has anything to do with spare shirt studs—

RENÉ (*who is delicately feeding himself while talking*): Don't be silly. It hasn't. I want to know – are you happy?

TREVOR: Immensely.

RENÉ (*disappointedly*): Are you? Why?

TREVOR: One never has any definite reason for being happy. It's simply a temperamental accident in most cases. I've nothing to worry me, no money troubles, no responsibilities; why should I be anything else but happy?

RENÉ: You ought to marry.

TREVOR: You think that would improve matters?

RENÉ: It would elevate you. Suffering is a great purifier.

TREVOR: You're not a very tempting advocate of matrimony.

RENÉ: I don't recommend it, except in desperate cases. Yours is distinctly a desperate case. You ought to marry, if only for your mother's sake.

TREVOR: My mother? I don't know that she is particularly anxious to see me mated just yet.

RENÉ: Your mother is one of those proud silent women who seldom indicate their wishes in actual words.

TREVOR: My dear René, my mother may be proud, but where her wishes are concerned she is not inclined to be silent.

RENÉ: At any rate, an unmarried son of marriageable age is always a great anxiety. There's never any knowing what impossible person he may fix his fancy on.

98

As old Lady Cloutsham said to me the other day, apropos of her eldest son: 'If Robert chooses a wife for himself, it's certain to be some demi-mondaine* with the merest superficial resemblance to a lady; whereas if I choose a wife for him I should select someone who at least would be a lady, with a merely superficial resemblance to a demi-mondaine.'

TREVOR: Poor Lady Cloutsham, her children are rather a trial to her, I imagine. Her youngest boy had to leave the country rather hurriedly, hadn't he?

RENÉ: Yes, poor dear. He's on a ranch somewhere in the wilds of Mexico. Conscience makes cowboys of us all. Unfortunately, it's other people's consciences that give all the trouble; there ought to be a law compelling everyone to keep his conscience under proper control, like chimneys that have to consume their own smoke. And then Gladys, who was the most hopeful member of the family, went and married a colonial bishop. That really finished Lady Cloutsham. As she said to me, 'I always classed colonial bishops with folk songs and peasant industries and all those things that one comes across at drawing-room meetings. I never expected to see them brought into one's family. This is what comes of letting young girls read Ibsen and Mrs Humphry Ward.'*

(*An unearthly long-drawn-out howl is heard.*)

TREVOR (*sitting up*): What on *earth*...?

RENÉ: Only the idiotic Drummond boy, who pretends he's the Hound of the Baskervilles.

(*Enter* AGATHA, *door left; runs giggling across stage pursued by* DRUMMOND *in sheet with phantom-hound mask on head. Exeunt both, door right back.*)

TREVOR (*rising slowly*): By Jove, I forgot I'd promised to go upstairs. Sybil will be fuming her head off.

RENÉ: We can't get a rubber of bridge* presently, can we?

TREVOR: 'Fraid not. The women would be rather mad if we shirked dancing.

(TREVOR *draws himself slowly together and lounges up staircase, left. Exits. Enter* SPARROWBY, *door right back.*)

SPARROWBY: Why aren't you rigged out like the rest of us, St Gall? (*Takes* TREVOR's *seat on couch.*)

RENÉ: Well, for one thing I'm in platonic mourning, having partially lost a mother, so it would hardly be the thing. And another reason is that the hood arrangement would ruffle one's hair so.

SPARROWBY: As if that mattered a bit. You're absurdly particular about your appearance and your clothes and how your tie is tied and about your hair. Look at me; it doesn't take me two minutes in the morning to do my hair.

RENÉ: So I should imagine. Isn't there a proverb – a fool and his hair are soon parted?

SPARROWBY: I say, you're beastly rude!

RENÉ: I know I am. My mother was a Whortleford, and the Whortlefords have no manners. I'm sorry I called you a fool, though, because I want you to do something really kind for me. Trevor has suggested a game

100

of bridge, and I don't want to back out of playing. The trouble is that I haven't a coin worth speaking about on me. If you'd be awfully pet-lamb and lend me something...?

SPARROWBY: I dislike lending on principle. It generally leads to unpleasantness.

RENÉ: Really, this worship of Mammon* is getting to be the curse of the age. People make more fuss about lending a few miserable guineas than the Sabine women did at being borrowed by the Romans.* I know a lady of somewhat mature age who took rather a fancy to me last season, and in a fit of sheer absence of mind she lent me ten pounds. She's got quite a comfortable income, but I declare she thinks more of that lost tenner than of the hundreds and hundreds that she's never lent me. It is become quite a mono-mania with her. It's her one subject of conversation whenever we meet.

SPARROWBY: Don't you intend paying her back?

RENÉ: Certainly not. Her loss makes her beautiful. It brings an effective touch of tragedy into an otherwise empty life. I could no more think of her apart from her mourned-for loan than one could think of Suez without the canal or Leda without the swan.*

SPARROWBY: If that's your view of your obligations I cer-tainly shan't lend you anything. By the way, where is Sybil Bomont? She's been sitting out about four dances with Trevor. It's about my turn now.

RENÉ (*with sudden energy*): Sybil has got a bad headache. She's lying down for a few minutes.

SPARROWBY: Where? I particularly want to see her.

RENÉ: In the billiard room, and she particularly doesn't want to see anyone.

SPARROWBY: But I only want—

(*Enter* CLARE *and* AGATHA, *door right back.*)

RENÉ: Agatha! Sparrowby is complaining that he's got no one to dance with.

AGATHA: Come along – they're just going to try that new Paris dance; I can't pronounce it.

SPARROWBY: But I can't dance it!

AGATHA: Neither can I. Come on.

SPARROWBY: But I say—

(*Exit* AGATHA, *dragging* SPARROWBY *off, door right back.*)

RENÉ: Thank goodness he's out of the way. People who make a principle of not lending money are social pests.

CLARE (*seating herself on couch*): This is going to be a dismal failure. By the way, have you seen Trevor anywhere?

RENÉ: Yes, he turned rather giddy with the dancing, I suppose, so he's taking a turn or two out in the air.

CLARE: Is he alone?

RENÉ: Oh, quite. So am I for the moment. Do stay and talk to me.

CLARE: You must be interesting, then. After sitting out successfully with Sparrowby and the two Drummond boys, I feel that there's nothing left in the way of dull and trivial conversation to listen to.

(While she is talking RENÉ *hands her half of the remaining peach and resumes his seat.)*

RENÉ: Let's talk about ourselves – that's always interesting.

CLARE: I suppose you mean, let's talk about yourself.

RENÉ: No, I'd much rather dissect your character; I find some good points in it.

CLARE: Do tell me what they are.

RENÉ: You have a rich aunt who is childless.

CLARE: She's a great-aunt.

RENÉ: All the better. That sort of thing doesn't spoil by being kept in the family for a generation or two. The greater the aunt the greater the prospect.

CLARE: And what other good points do you find in me?

RENÉ: I think I've nearly exhausted the list.

CLARE: I don't find you a bit interesting.

RENÉ: Well, be patient for a moment; I'm going to say something quite personal and interesting. Will you marry me? The question is sudden, I admit, but these things are best done suddenly. I suppose it was the mention of your great-aunt that suggested it.

CLARE: The answer is equally sudden. It's 'No.'

RENÉ: Are you quite sure you mean that?

CLARE: Convinced.

RENÉ: How thoroughly sensible of you. So many girls in your place would have said yes.

CLARE: I dare say. Our sex hasn't much reputation for discrimination. I didn't know that marrying was in your line.

RENÉ: It isn't. I dislike the idea of wives about a house: they accumulate dust. Besides, so few of the really nice women in my set could afford to marry me.

CLARE: From the point of view of reputation?

RENÉ: Oh, I wasn't thinking of that. At twenty-three one is supposed to have conquered every earthly passion; of course it's the fashion in statesmanship nowadays to allow the conquered to have the upper hand.

CLARE: A convenient fashion, and saves a lot of bother. Tell me, taking me apart from my great-aunt, are you pleased to consider that I should make a satisfactory wife?

RENÉ: Satisfactory wives aren't made, they're invented. Chiefly by married men. But as things go I think we should have made what is called a well-assorted couple. I should have taught you in time to be as thoroughly selfish as myself, and then each would have looked after our own particular interests without having need to fear that the other was likely to suffer from any neglect.

CLARE: There is much to be said for that point of view. It's the imperfectly selfish souls that cause themselves and others so many heart-burnings. People who make half-sacrifices for others always find that it's the unfinished half that's being looked at. Naturally they come to regard themselves as unappreciated martyrs.

RENÉ: By the way, I may as well tell you before you find out. Trevor isn't out of doors. He's sitting out with Sybil somewhere on the landing.

CLARE (*half rising from seat*): You beast! Why did you tell me he'd gone out?

RENÉ: Well, the fact of the matter is I thought that if those two were left together undisturbed for half an hour or so, one or other of them might propose.

CLARE (*resuming seat*): Oh, that's the game, is it? And has Sybil enlisted your services in this precious stalking movement?

RENÉ: Oh, dear, no: I'm merely working in a good cause. Someone's got to marry Trevor, you know, and the sooner the better. Personally, I don't think it's very hopeful, but the whole motive of this otherwise idiotic dance is to head Trevor into a matrimonial ambush of some sort. He's so superbly sleepy that there's just a chance of it coming off, but I'm not sanguine.

CLARE: If he *is* to be rushed into marrying someone, I don't see why I shouldn't be in the running as well as anyone else.

RENÉ: Exactly what William was saying to me this morning.

CLARE: William! The pageboy?

RENÉ: Yes, he's rather keen on seeing you Mrs Trevor Bavvel.

CLARE: That's very sweet of him, but I didn't know he took such an intelligent interest in the matter.

RENÉ: It's not altogether disinterested. It seems they've got a half-crown sweepstake on the event in the servants' hall, and he happened to draw you, so naturally he's in a bit of a flutter on your behalf.

CLARE: I didn't know we were the centre of so much speculation. Mercy on us, what would Hortensia say if she knew that she was nurturing a living sweepstake under her roof! And is William good enough to consider that I have a fair sporting chance of pulling it off?

RENÉ: I fancy he's rather despondent. He said you didn't seem to try as hard as some of the others were doing. He puts your chair as near Trevor's as possible at prayers, but that's all he's able to do personally.

CLARE: The little devil!

RENÉ: I believe that if the Vulpy woman wasn't handicapped with a preliminary husband, she'd carry Trevor off against all competitors. She's just got the bounce that appeals to a lazy, slow-witted bachelor.

CLARE: There's something I particularly object to in that woman. She always talks to me with just a suspicion of a furtive sneer in her voice that I find extremely irritating. I don't know why Agatha inflicted her on us.

(*Enter* AGATHA, *right back.*)

AGATHA: What's that you're saying about me?

CLARE: Only wondering what induced you to cart Mrs Vulpy down here.

AGATHA: Oh, come, she's not a bad soul, you know, taking her all round. (*Seats herself on couch.*) We are all of us as God made us.

RENÉ: In Mrs Vulpy's case some recognition is due to her maid as a collaborator.

AGATHA: You're all very ill-natured about her. Anyway, this dance was her idea.

CLARE: Yes, and a horrid mess it's going to land us all in. I daren't think of tomorrow. By the afternoon the news will have spread over the greater part of Somersetshire that a costume ball has been given at Briony in the temporary absence of Mrs Bavvel.

AGATHA: I say, do you think she'll be very furious?

CLARE: If Hortensia is more intolerant on one question than on any other, it's on the subject of what she calls 'mixed dancing'. I remember a county fête at Crowcoombe

106

where she vetoed the project of a maypole dance by children of six and seven years old until absolutely assured that the sexes would dance apart. Some of the smaller children were rather ambiguously dressed and were too shy to tell us their names, and the curate and I had a long and delicate task in sorting the hes from the shes. One four-year-old baffled our most patient researches, and finally had to dance by itself round a maypole of its own.

AGATHA: I'm beginning to get dreadfully frightened about tomorrow. Can't we water it down a bit and pretend that we had games and Sir Roger de Coverley* and that sort of thing?

CLARE: We shall have to tone things down as much as possible, but Hortensia will hold an inquiry into the whole matter, and drag the truth out by inches. She'll probably dismiss half the servants and have the morning room repapered; as for us—

RENÉ: There's a very good up train* at 3.15.

AGATHA: But I haven't made arrangements for going anywhere; it will be most inconvenient.

CLARE: On the morrow of an unsuccessful coup d'état one generally travels first and makes one's arrangements afterwards.

(*A prolonged howl heard.*)

RENÉ: The idiotic Drummond boy again.

(*Enter* DRUMMOND, *door right back.*)

DRUMMOND: I say, you make nice cheerful hosts, sitting there like a lot of moping owls. Do come and buck things up a bit; there are only two couples dancing.

RENÉ (*tragically*): Yes, let us go and dance on the edge of our volcano.

AGATHA: Oh, don't – I feel quite creepy. It reminds me of that Duchess person's ball on the eve of Waterloo.*

(*Exeunt* DRUMMOND, RENÉ, AGATHA, *door right back.* CLARE *remains seated. Enter* MRS VULPY, *centre.*)

MRS VULPY: All alone, Miss Henessey? By the way, where is that dear boy, Trevor?

CLARE: I believe he's upstairs, and I don't think he wishes to be disturbed.

MRS VULPY: I suppose that means that you are waiting to catch him when he comes down, and that *you* don't want to be disturbed.

CLARE: Oh, please put that construction on it if it amuses you. I shouldn't like to think you weren't enjoying yourself.

MRS VULPY: Oh, I'm enjoying myself right enough, Miss Henessey, watching some of the little byplay that's goin' on. (*Seats herself.*) It is *Miss* Henessey, isn't it? (*Gives a little laugh.*)

CLARE: What do you mean?

MRS VULPY: Oh, well, only that we've met before, you know – at least, I've seen you before, though you probably didn't see me. You were writing your name in the visitors' book at the Grand Anchor Hotel at Bristol, just about six weeks ago.

CLARE: I did stop there one night about six weeks ago. I don't remember seeing you there.

MRS VULPY: I remember not only seeing you, but the names you wrote in the book; 'Henessey' wasn't one of them, nor 'Miss' anything, either.

CLARE: How clever of you to remember. You seem to have a good head for business – other people's business.

MRS VULPY: Oh, well, I suppose it was the innocent vagueness of the names you had put down that arrested my attention. 'Mr and Mrs Smith, London.' Your companion had gone upstairs with the luggage, so I didn't see Mr Smith, and somehow at the time I had a feeling that I wasn't seeing Mrs Smith – at least, not the permanent Mrs Smith.

CLARE: It sounds rather crude and compromising as you put it, I admit, but the explanation is not really very dreadful. Only—

MRS VULPY: Only you don't feel disposed to give an explanation at such short notice? You're quite right. Second thoughts are usually more convincing in such cases.

CLARE: Well, to be candid, I don't see that my travelling adventures are any particular concern of yours.

MRS VULPY: Perhaps you're right. I dare say they more immediately concern the lady whose guest you are. Shall I raise her curiosity on the subject? As you've got such a satisfactory explanation ready, you can have no objection, I suppose?

CLARE: You know Mrs Bavvel well enough to know that what might seem a harmless escapade to ordinary judges would not be regarded so leniently by her.

MRS VULPY: And Mr Trevor? He doesn't share his mother's prejudices. You won't mind if I let him into our little secret about the Smith ménage?

CLARE (*rising from her seat*): Mrs Vulpy, what particular gratification do you find in threatening to make mischief between me and my friends? It shows you up in rather a bad light, and I don't really see what you expect to gain by it.

MRS VULPY: Simply, my dear girl, we happen to be interested in the same man.

CLARE: You mean Trevor?

MRS VULPY: Of course. I know perfectly well that all you girls are hanging round here for a chance of snapping him up, and I'm clever enough to see which of you is likely to succeed. It won't be Sybil Bomont, whatever anyone may say.

CLARE: In any case, you can scarcely regard yourself as a competitor.

MRS VULPY: Because of being already married, you mean? Well, I don't mind telling you I've more definite news about my husband's condition than I've been pretending to have. He was past all chance of recovery when the last mail went out. I'm too honest to pretend to be anything but glad. If you knew the life we've had! I've been a lonely woman since the day I married Peter, and now I don't intend being lonely any more. As soon as I set eyes on Trevor Bavvel I knew he was just the sort of man I wanted to begin life with over again.

CLARE: And do you suppose that you are so obviously *his* conception of the ideal life-mate that he'll throw himself at your feet as soon as he knows you are free to marry him?

MRS VULPY: Oh, my dear, most things in life that are worth having have to be worked for. I've made a good beginning by enlisting his sympathy as a fellow conspirator over this dance. The worse row we get into over it the better. Then, when my husband's estate has been straightened out, I shan't be badly off, and I shall come to this neighbourhood and do a little hunting and give bridge parties and all that sort of thing. Provided nothing happens in the meantime, I fancy I stand a very fair chance of pulling it off.

CLARE: I see.

MRS VULPY: Ah, you do see, do you? You understand now why I want your flirtation with Trevor to be nipped in the bud, and why I'm prepared to nip it myself if necessary with that little story of the Grand Anchor Hotel?

CLARE: You are making one little miscalculation, Mrs Vulpy. Trevor was a public-school boy, and in English public-school tradition the spy and the tale-bearer don't occupy a very exalted position.

MRS VULPY: Oh, you may call me hard names, but you can't wriggle away from me in that fashion. I've got you in my grip! So, either you leave the field clear for me or the story of your visit to the Grand Anchor Hotel with a gentleman – whom, for want of fuller information, we will call Mr Smith – becomes public property.

CLARE: Someone is coming downstairs. Shall we go and see how the dancing is going on? They're playing that Bulgarian march.

MRS VULPY: Oh, yes, let's go and hear it. I love Slav music
  — it takes one out of oneself so.
CLARE: Which is sometimes an advantage.

(*Exeunt* MRS VULPY *and* CLARE. *Enter down staircase, left,*
SYBIL *and* TREVOR.)

TREVOR: I say, it's getting nearly time to call this off.
SYBIL: Oh, nonsense, it's only just ten. They can't be back
  before eleven. Your mother is delivering an address,
  and she's not given to cutting her words short on these
  occasions, I believe.
TREVOR: Well, half an hour more, then. And let's make it go
  with a bit more fling for the wind-up.
SYBIL: Right-oh!

(*Enter* SPARROWBY, *left.*)

  Lord, here's that pestering idiot again.
SPARROWBY: Ah, at last I've found you! Are you better?
SYBIL: Better?
SPARROWBY: I was told you were lying down in the billiard
  room with a bad headache.
SYBIL: Who on earth told you that?
SPARROWBY: St Gall.
SYBIL: Oh, René! Never believe a word he says. I'm in my
  usual health, but I'm frightfully hungry. Trevor, do go
  and forage for something edible. I'll wait for you here.
  I was too excited to eat much at dinner, and I know
  I shan't dare to come down to breakfast tomorrow.
TREVOR: I'll go and parley with Cook. (*Exit, door centre.*)

SPARROWBY: What have you been doing all this time?

SYBIL (*seating herself on couch*): Oh, don't ask me. Sitting upstairs with Trevor and trying to keep him from going to sleep. I assure you it wasn't amusing.

SPARROWBY: I should never want to go to sleep if I were by your side.

SYBIL: What an inconvenient husband you would be.

SPARROWBY: Oh, I wish you wouldn't be always fooling. (*Seats himself beside her.*) You don't know how much I love you!

SYBIL: Of course I don't; I've only got your word for it that you care in the least bit for me. Now, if you were to do something to prove it—

SPARROWBY: I'd do anything.

SYBIL: Well, do something that would give you a name in the world. For instance, paint pictures and have them exhibited in the Royal Academy: it would be something to talk about when one went there.

SPARROWBY: But I can't paint.

SYBIL: Oh, I don't think that matters, as long as you exhibited. Of course, they wouldn't sell. Or why not found a religion, like Muhammad and Wesley and those sort of people did?

SPARROWBY: But you can't found religions off-hand. You want inspiration and enthusiasm and disciples, and all manner of special conditions.

SYBIL: Well, then, you could invent a new system of scoring at county cricket, or breed a new variety of fox terrier.

SPARROWBY: But it would take years and years to produce a new variety.

SYBIL: I would wait – oh, so patiently.

SPARROWBY: *Sybil*, if I was successful in breeding a new kind of fox terrier, would you really marry me?

SYBIL: I wouldn't exactly marry you, but I would buy some of the puppies from you. I've got an awfully jolly little fox terrier at home. If you tell her 'The Kaiser's coming,' or 'Roosevelt's coming,' she lies quite still, but if you say, 'King Edward's coming,' she jumps up at once. Isn't it clever? I taught her myself with gingerbread biscuits.

SPARROWBY: Won't you realise that I'm asking you to be my wife?

SYBIL: Of course I realise it – you've asked me so often that I'm getting to expect nothing else. I wish you would vary it a little and ask me something different. Only, don't ask me that dreadful thing about 'this man's father was my father's only son' – it nearly gives me brain fever.

SPARROWBY: I wonder if you have a heart at all!

SYBIL: Of course I've got the usual fittings. It's very rude of you to suggest that I'm jerry-built.* But look here, joking apart, do do something to oblige me. Go and dance with poor Evelyn Bray – she's been at the piano all the evening and hasn't had a scrap of dancing herself.

SPARROWBY: If I do, will you give me a dance afterwards?

SYBIL: I'll give you two.

SPARROWBY (*rising from his seat*): You angel. I wish you'd always be as kind. (*Exit, door right back.*)

SYBIL (*hearing someone coming*): Is that you, Trevor? I'm getting ravenous.

(*Enter* AGATHA, *door centre.*)

Oh, Lord!

AGATHA: Hullo, Sybil, have you seen Trevor?

SYBIL: No, I think he's dancing.

AGATHA: He hasn't been in the dancing room for about an hour; neither have you. (*Seats herself on chair right of couch.*)

SYBIL: I'm so hot I'm sitting out here to get cool. I suppose it's the excitement. I say, do go and help Evelyn at the piano – she's getting quite fagged out, poor child.

AGATHA (*acidly*): I've just played them a polka; Evelyn hasn't been near the piano for the last half-hour. If you hadn't been sticking to Trevor like a drowning leech you might have known that.

SYBIL (*furiously*): I haven't been sticking on him, and leeches don't drown, anyway.

AGATHA: Oh, I'm not up in their natural history. I only know they stick like mud. I'll say a floating leech if you like.

SYBIL: It so happens I've been listening to marriage proposals from that pestering Sparrowby all the evening.

AGATHA: I've had the infliction of dancing with him no fewer than four times, my dear, and he kept on complaining that he couldn't find you. Don't be disheartened: accidents will happen to the most accomplished fibbers.

SYBIL: Why is it that plain women are always so venomous?

AGATHA: Oh, if you're going to be introspective, my dear. (*Laughs.*)

(*Enter* TREVOR, *door centre.*)

TREVOR: All I could raise was some cold rice pudding and a bottle of pickled walnuts. If there's anything I detest in this world it's rice pudding.

AGATHA (*going over to table*): I loathe rice pudding – it's so wholesome. On the other hand, I simply adore pickled walnuts. (*Helps herself.*)

TREVOR: Won't you have some, Sybil? (*Helps himself.*)

SYBIL (*rising from seat*): I'm not going to stay here to be insulted. I've been called a liar and a leech.

AGATHA: I said fibber, my dear, not liar.

(*Exit* SYBIL, *door right back.*)

TREVOR: Have you two been having a slanging match?

AGATHA: Oh, no, only poor Sybil is so dreadfully short-tempered, she can't take anything in good part. She's a dear, sweet girl, one of the very best, but I should be awfully sorry for any fellow who married her. That reminds me, Trevor – you ought to marry. (*Helps herself to another walnut.*)

TREVOR: There's a great deal to be said for that point of view; and as far as I can see there's no particular likelihood of it's being left unsaid. (*Helps himself to walnut.*)

AGATHA: I suppose the difficulty is to think of anyone you care for sufficiently.

TREVOR: Have you anything to say against Mrs Vulpy?

AGATHA: Good heavens! Mrs Vulpy? That vulgar, over-dressed parrot, with the manners of a cockney

116

sparrow? I should think she began life in a Cheap Jack store.* Surely you can't be thinking seriously of her?

TREVOR: I asked you if you had anything to say against her. Considering the short notice you managed very well. Wasn't it you who brought her down here?

AGATHA (*helping herself to walnut*): Well, yes, I suppose I did. Somehow in Folkestone she didn't seem such an awful rotter. Anyway, she's got a husband. No, the woman for you must be one with great similarity of tastes—

TREVOR: On the contrary, I avoid that kind. At the present moment I regard you with something bordering on aversion. (*Stirs frantically in jar.*)

AGATHA: Regard me with aversion! My dear Trevor!

TREVOR: If it hadn't been for our duplicate passion for pickled walnuts this cruel tragedy wouldn't have happened. There's not one left.

AGATHA: Oh, Trevor, not one? (*Stirs mournfully in jar.*)

TREVOR: No, the woman I marry must have an unbridled appetite for rice pudding.

AGATHA (*dubiously*): I dare say some rice pudding, nicely cooked, wouldn't be bad eating. (*Begins agitating spoon listlessly through rice pudding dish.*)

TREVOR: That is not the spirit in which my ideal woman must approach rice pudding. She must eat it with an avidity that will almost create scandal; she must devour it secretly in dark corners, she must buy it in small quantities from chemists on the plea that she has neuralgia. Such a woman I could be happy with.

AGATHA: She might be odious in other respects. (*While talking is waving spoon in air.*)

TREVOR: One must not expect to find perfection.

AGATHA: I wish you would be serious when we are discussing a serious subject. I suppose matrimony is a more serious affair for us poor women than for you men.

TREVOR: How can I discuss anything seriously when you're covering me with fragments of rice pudding?

AGATHA: Oh, you poor dear, I'm so sorry. Let me rub you down.

TREVOR: No, don't you; I won't be massaged with rice pudding.

(*Enter* MRS VULPY, *door centre.*)

MRS VULPY: What *are* you two people playing at?

TREVOR: Only trying to find new uses for cold rice pudding. I was firmly convinced as a child that it couldn't be primarily intended as a food.

MRS VULPY: René is just going to do his nautch-girl dance. He wants you to go and play tom-tom music, Agatha.

AGATHA: Bother René. Why was I born good-natured? (*Exit right.*)

TREVOR: Stay and talk to me, Mrs Vulpy. I've seen the nautch dance before.

MRS VULPY: You are such a sought-after young man that I feel I oughtn't to be taking you away from the others.

TREVOR: I'd rather sit and talk with you than with any of the others.

MRS VULPY: Dear me! I thought you never worked up the energy to make pretty speeches.

TREVOR: I don't; it's my mere sheer laziness that makes me blurt out the truth on this occasion.

MRS VULPY: And am I really to suppose that it is truth that you would rather sit with me than with any of the others?

TREVOR: You are the only woman of the lot that it is safe to sit out with. Perhaps you are not very securely married, but you're not exactly floating loose ready to take advantage of the artless innocence of a young bachelor.

MRS VULPY: And is that where my superior fascination begins and leaves off?

TREVOR: That's where it begins. I didn't say it left off there.

MRS VULPY: Now don't try to talk pretty. You know you're not capable of sustained effort in that direction. Nothing is more discouraging than to have a man say that you've ruined his life, and then to find that you haven't even given him after-dinner insomnia.

TREVOR: Oh, I promise to keep awake – only it's rather soothing and sedative to talk to a charming woman who has no intention of marrying one. You don't intend to marry me, do you?

MRS VULPY: My dear Trevor, I have intended marrying you ever since I first saw you.

TREVOR: They say the road to matrimony is paved with good intentions, don't they?

MRS VULPY: I have heard it put in a more roundabout manner.

TREVOR: In your case isn't there rather a big obstacle in the road?

MRS VULPY: You mean Peter?

TREVOR: I suppose he *is* a factor in the situation?

MRS VULPY: Of course he's my husband, and it's my duty to think of him before anyone else, but I am not going to be a hypocrite and waste sentiment in that direction. Our married life has been about as odious an experience as I wish to go through.

119

TREVOR: Still, I suppose even an unsatisfactory marriage has to be taken into account. There is no first offender's clause in our marriage system. However uncongenial he may be, Peter remains your husband.

MRS VULPY: Well, that's the question. Peter was always selfish, but double pneumonia on the top of nervous breakdown may have overcome even his obstinate temperament. Why, at any moment I might get what I should be obliged to call in public 'bad news'. So you see, I'm not so safe a person to sit and make pretty speeches to as you thought. And now I suppose my fascination has melted into thin air?

TREVOR: No, I shall merely have to label you 'dangerous', along with the others.

MRS VULPY: Ah, Trevor, I'm much more dangerous than any of the others, if you only knew it.

TREVOR: Why so?

MRS VULPY: Because I really want you for your own self. The others are all after you for family reasons and general convenience and that sort of thing. I want you because... well, I've seen a bit of the world, and I know the worth of a man like you, who can't be flattered or humbugged or led by the nose—

TREVOR: Hush! Someone's coming.

(*Enter* WILLIAM, *door left.*)

Just clear these things away, William; I should like my mother to find the hall in its usual state. Now, Mrs Vulpy, I must be going in to the dance. I've shirked my duty most horribly.

MRS VULPY: Well, let's have a dreamy waltz together, to set the seal on what we've been talking about. We are friends, aren't we?

(*Exeunt* TREVOR *and* MRS VULPY, *door right.* WILLIAM *gathers up empty plates. Enter* RENÉ, *door centre.*)

RENÉ (*helping himself to wine*): William, can you find me any more peaches?

WILLIAM: No, sir, I brought you the last.

RENÉ (*arranging himself comfortably on couch*): Well, try to discover a fig or banana somewhere, do; and if you remind me tomorrow I'll ask Mr Ludovic to give you that yellow striped waistcoat that he hardly ever wears.

WILLIAM: Thank you, sir. You don't know of no one wanting a page, do you, sir?

RENÉ: Why, are you thinking of leaving?

WILLIAM: I expect I shall have to leave without having time to do any thinking about it, sir. When Mrs Bavvel comes to hear about our goings-on behind her back she'll behave like one of those cyclops that sweeps away whole villages.

RENÉ: Cyclone, William, not cyclops.

WILLIAM: That's it, sir, cyclone, and I expect I shall be among the sweepings. I've no particular fancy to be going home out of a situation just now, sir. Home life is a different thing with you gentry, you're so comfortable and heathen.

RENÉ: When one comes think of it, I suppose we are. It's a rather overcrowded profession, all the same.

(*While* WILLIAM *is talking* RENÉ *is helping himself to* TREVOR's *Russian cigarettes and filling his case.*)

WILLIAM: Ah, sir, *you* haven't known what it was to be
     brought up by respectable parents.

RENÉ: Really, William!

WILLIAM: My father is Plymouth Brethren,* sir. Not that
     I've anything to say against Plymouth as a religion, but
     in a small cottage it takes up a lot of room. My father
     believed in smiting sin wherever he found it; what I
     complained of was that he always seemed to find it
     in the same place. Plymouth narrows the prospective.
     Between gentry religion and cottage religion there's the
     same difference as between keeping ferrets and living in
     a hutch with one.

(*Exit* WILLIAM, *door centre. Enter the first four in couples by
door right back,* TREVOR *and* MRS VULPY, DRUMMOND *and*
CLARE, *and* SYBIL, SPARROWBY *and* AGATHA, *prancing
through hall and singing* 'Non je ne marcherai pas',* *which is
heard being played on piano off.*)

AGATHA (*to* RENÉ): You slacker! Come and join in.

(*They exeunt in same order through door left, still singing.*)

RENÉ (*to himself*): I'm of far too tidy a disposition to leave
     half-emptied bottles lying about. Did I hear wheels?
     (*Rises and listens.*) Stop your squalling, you people.
     I fancied I heard wheels. (*Listens again.*) My nerves are
     getting quite jumpy. (*Reseats himself.*)

(*Hall door right thrown open. Enter* HORTENSIA, *who turns to someone in porch.*)

HORTENSIA: Ludovic, quick, catch the carriage; I've left my pamphlets and notes in it. (*Catches sight of* RENÉ, *who is regarding her with helpless stare.*) Mr St Gall! May I ask what you are doing here at this hour?

RENÉ: Such a silly mistake. Old Colonel Nicholas asked me to go over to Bowerwood after dinner, as I was all alone. I distinctly told the groom Bowerwood, but he drove me here instead, and I didn't see where I was till he had driven off. So I've had to wait here till he comes to fetch me.

HORTENSIA (*who has been staring fixedly at him and at the wine bottles and siphons on the table*): Will you repeat your story, please? I didn't quite follow.

RENÉ: Colonel Nicholas, thinking I might be lonely—

HORTENSIA: I hear music!

RENÉ: I've been thinking I heard harps in the air all the evening. I put it down to the state of my nerves.

(SYBIL, *with hood over head, runs through, laughing, from door left, and exits door centre, without noticing* HORTENSIA.)

Ah! Did you see *that*? Did you see *that*?

(HORTENSIA *stares at doorway where figure vanished. Howl heard off. Enter* DRUMMOND *with phantom hound mask on, door left, runs through and exits centre.*)

Oh, say something, or we shall... both... go... mad! (*Sobs convulsively.*)

HORTENSIA (*furiously*): Ludovic!

(*Enter* LUDOVIC, *hall door right.*)

LUDOVIC: What is happening?

(RENÉ *has collapsed in fit of pretended hysterics in armchair.*)

HORTENSIA: The boy is either drunk or mad! Something
    disgraceful is taking place in this house!

LUDOVIC: Something disgraceful, here? René, what *is* all
    this?

RENÉ (*sitting rigid in chair and staring straight in front of
    him*): Only werewolves chasing goblins to the sound
    of unearthly music. Will someone kindly see if my
    carriage has come? I refuse to stay another moment
    in this house.

(*Enter* TREVOR, CLARE, MRS VULPY *from door left,* SYBIL *and*
DRUMMOND, *door centre, all unhooded.*)

TREVOR: Oh, good God!

(RENÉ *pours out glass of wine and drains it, then lies back com-
posedly in his chair. A prolonged pause, during which* HORTENSIA
surveys sheepish group of revellers.)

SYBIL (*weakly*): We were having games.

MRS VULPY: Old English games.

DRUMMOND: Charades.

CLARE: Historical charades.

SYBIL
TREVOR
MRS VULPY
DRUMMOND
} (*together*): Yes, historical charades.

(*Enter* AGATHA *and* SPARROWBY, *door right back, prancing in together, singing with fatuous exuberance,* 'Non je ne marcherai pas.' *They stop, horror-stricken, in centre of stage.*)

HORTENSIA (*seating herself in high-backed chair, her voice trembling with rage*): May I ask who has organised this abominable and indecent orgy in my house? Will somebody enlighten me?

CLARE: It was something we got up on the spur of the moment; there was nothing organised.

HORTENSIA: And what brought people in from outside? I've heard a contemptibly ridiculous story about Mr St Gall's accidental arrival here; how do you account for Mr Drummond's presence? Was he also trying to make his way to Bowerwood?

DRUMMOND (*blunderingly*): Yes.

RENÉ (*decisively*): No, that's my story. I won't be plagiarised.

SYBIL: He dropped in by chance.

DRUMMOND: Yes, quite by chance.

HORTENSIA: Also on the spur of the moment! A moment, be it observed, when I happened to be temporarily absent. And, knowing my strong objection to the questionable form of entertainment involved in promiscuous dancing, you choose this moment for indulging in an aggravated and indecent kind of dance which I can only describe as a brawl.

MRS VULPY: But, dear Mrs Bavvel, I assure you there is nothing indecent in a sheet-and-pillowcase dance. Lulu Duchess of Dulverton gave one at—

HORTENSIA: Lulu Duchess of Dulverton is not a person whose behaviour or opinions will be taken as a pattern at Briony as long as I am mistress here. While you are still under my roof, Mrs Vulpy, I trust you will endeavour to remember that fact. Whether, after this deplorable error of taste, you will see fit to prolong your visit, of course, I don't know. Apparently this monstrous misuse of the bed linen which is intended for the sleeping accommodation of my guests was carried out at your suggestion.

MRS VULPY (*bursting into tears*): I think, considering the mental anxiety and strain through which I am passing, with a husband hovering between Johannesburg and heaven, I'm being most unfairly treated. (*Exit, door left.*)

HORTENSIA: I've refrained from complaining, Agatha, at the inconsiderate way in which you bring brambles and hedge weeds and garden refuse into the house, but I must protest against your introducing individuals of the type of Mrs Vulpy as guests at Briony. Who is that playing the piano?

SYBIL: I think it's Evelyn Bray.

HORTENSIA: Ah! Who also dropped in accidentally, I suppose? Ludovic, will you kindly tell Miss Bray that we don't require any more music this evening.

(*Exit* LUDOVIC, *door right back.*)

Had we not returned unexpectedly early, I presume this outrageous entertainment would have been kept from my knowledge. I may inform you that the mayor took it upon himself to cancel the reception at the town hall at which I was to have delivered a brief address, for the rather far-fetched reason of showing respect and sympathy at the sudden disappearance of Mrs St Gall.

RENÉ: I say! That was rather pet-lamb of him.

HORTENSIA: Mrs St Gall's son appears to treat the incident as of less serious importance.

RENÉ: I came here for rest and sympathy, with the faint possibility of a little bridge to distract my thoughts; I wasn't to be expected to know that historical charades would be going on all round me. My nerves won't recover for weeks.

HORTENSIA: I am a persistent advocate of the abolition of corporal punishment in the navy and in board schools,* but I must confess, Mr St Gall, that a good birching inflicted on you would cause me no displeasure.

RENÉ: A most indelicate wind-up to a doubtful evening's amusement. I should insist on its being done in camera.*

(*Enter* LUDOVIC, *door right back.*)

SYBIL: Really, Mrs Bavvel, we must plead guilty to having planned this semi-impromptu affair just a little, but we thought it would be such a good occasion for making an announcement.

AGATHA: An announcement?

HORTENSIA: What announcement?

SYBIL (*looking at* TREVOR): An announcement that I'm provisionally... well, engaged—

SPARROWBY: Oh, Sybil, you angel! Let me announce it! Sybil and I are engaged!

LUDOVIC: Engaged? You and Sybil? Impossible. I congratulate you, of course, but it's... most unexpected.

CLARE: You dear thing. Congratulations.

SYBIL (*furiously*): You misunderstand me. I'm not engaged! Do you hear?

SPARROWBY: Oh, Sybil, but you just said you were!

SYBIL: You fool! I was talking about something quite different. (*Exit, door left.*)

HORTENSIA: There seems to be some confusion about this wonderful announcement.

LUDOVIC: I gathered that Miss Bomont was talking about something she's engaged on. Anyhow, she distinctly stated that she is not engaged to Mr Sparrowby.

HORTENSIA: In any case, this is hardly a fortunate moment in which to make announcements of secondary interest.

(*Enter* WILLIAM, *door centre, carrying plate with banana. Stops, horrified, on seeing* MRS BAVVEL, *who rises from chair.*)

What are you carrying there, William?

WILLIAM (*miserably*): A banana, ma'am.

HORTENSIA: What are you doing with a banana at this time of night?

WILLIAM: It's for her – him – the cockatoo, ma'am.

HORTENSIA: For Adolphus? At a quarter to eleven! He's never fed at this hour.

WILLIAM: She – he – seemed disturbed and restless, as if he was asking for something, ma'am.

HORTENSIA: Disturbed? I am not surprised. In the fourteen years that he has lived here he has never before experienced such an evening of disgraceful disorder. Trevor, perhaps you will see that your neighbours who dropped in so unexpectedly will leave with as little delay as possible. Those of you who are at present my guests will kindly retire to their sleeping apartments. William!

WILLIAM: Yes, ma'am?

HORTENSIA: Tell Cook to send a cold supper for myself and Mr Ludovic to the dining room. Some beef and pickled walnuts and a few peaches.

WILLIAM (*weakly*): Yes, ma'am.

HORTENSIA: Tomorrow I shall have a good deal to say on the subject of these deplorable proceedings. Tonight I am too upset. I left Briony an orderly English home; I return to find it a casino.

(*Exit* HORTENSIA *up staircase left, followed by* LUDOVIC, *who holds up his hands in mock despair. The others stand blankly watching them disappear.* RENÉ *seizes banana which* WILLIAM *is holding on plate and exits right eating it. He is followed by* DRUMMOND *and* AGATHA. WILLIAM *exits, door left, leaving* CLARE *and* TREVOR *alone.*)

ACT III

Breakfast room at Briony Manor.

LUDOVIC, *having just breakfasted, is still seated, chair pushed back from table, reading paper.* BUTLER *about to clear away breakfast things.*

BUTLER: Shall I remove the breakfast things, sir?

LUDOVIC (*glancing at clock*): Is no one else coming down? Where is Miss Clare?

BUTLER: Miss Clare complained of a headache, sir, and had breakfast in her room.

LUDOVIC: And Mr Trevor?

BUTLER: Mr Trevor breakfasted very early and went up to the farm. Miss Sybil breakfasted in her room.

LUDOVIC: Had she a headache also?

BUTLER: She complained of a headache, sir. Mrs Vulpy breakfasted in her room.

LUDOVIC: The same... complaint?

BUTLER: No, sir, anxiety and nervous depression. She made a very big breakfast, sir. I don't know whether Miss Agatha has had her breakfast sent up. She wasn't awake half an hour ago.

LUDOVIC: By the way, do you know whether Mrs Vulpy received any telegrams this morning?

BUTLER: She received one, sir, that she seemed to be expecting.

LUDOVIC: Ah!

BUTLER: She held it for a long while looking at it, sir, theatrical like, and then said there was no answer.

LUDOVIC: Did she seem less depressed after she'd received it?

BUTLER: She ordered some more kidneys and toast. I should say she was a lot more cheerful.

(*Enter* AGATHA *hastily, door left.*)

AGATHA: Hullo, Ludovic, only you here? I meant to have breakfast upstairs, but I saw Hortensia go out to the rose garden, so I skipped down.

BUTLER: Shall I warm some of the breakfast dishes for you, miss?

AGATHA: No, just make me some fresh tea, and leave the ham and sardines. (*While speaking has both arms on the table.*) I don't see any butter.

BUTLER: Your sleeve's in the butter, miss.*

AGATHA: Oh, so it is. And you might bring in some more toast.

BUTLER: Yes, miss.

AGATHA: Isn't there any honey?

LUDOVIC: Your other sleeve is in the honey.

AGATHA: Oh, bother.

(*Exit* BUTLER, *door centre.*)

I say, did you breakfast with Hortensia? Was she very awful?

LUDOVIC: She told me she had lain awake most of the night boiling with indignation. She's now in the hard-boiled state of cold vindictiveness.

AGATHA: Mercy on us! Whatever shall we do?

LUDOVIC: Personally I intend going for a few weeks on a visit to Ireland.

AGATHA: But we can't all go to Ireland.

LUDOVIC: One of the great advantages of Ireland as a place of residence is that a large number of excellent people never go there.

AGATHA: You're disgustingly selfish – you don't think what is to become of the rest of us.

LUDOVIC: On the contrary, it's you that are selfish and inconsiderate. If one of you would only marry Trevor, all this Hortensia discomfort and forced marching would be avoided.

AGATHA: But how absurd you are, Ludovic! One can't marry Trevor without his consent. No really nice girl would make advances to a man unless he showed himself attracted to her first; and, as regards Trevor, it wouldn't be the slightest good, anyway; one might as well make advances to the landscape. We poor women are so dreadfully handicapped. If I were only a man—

LUDOVIC: If you were a man you couldn't marry Trevor, so that wouldn't help us. Your sleeve's in the honey again.

(*Enter* BUTLER, *door centre, with tea and toast.*)

BUTLER: Is there anything else I can bring you, miss?

AGATHA: No, thank you. Oh, tell Cook, in case I should be travelling later in the day, to cut me some ham sandwiches. No mustard.

BUTLER: Yes, miss. Shall you want the dogcart ordered?

LUDOVIC: You had better say the wagonette and the luggage cart; there may be others leaving this afternoon.

BUTLER: The 3.20 up or the 4.15 down, miss?*

AGATHA: I'm not quite sure. I'll let you know later.

BUTLER: Yes, miss. (*Exit, door centre.*)

AGATHA: If Hortensia is in a never-darken-my-doors-again kind of temper I shall go right off to town and on somewhere from there. On the other hand, if it's the kind of outbreak that blows over in a week or two, I shall merely go and stay with some people I know at Exeter.

LUDOVIC: Nice people?

AGATHA: Oh, dear, no. Quite uninteresting. I met them somewhere in Switzerland; they helped to find some luggage that had gone astray. I always lose luggage when I travel. They have porridge in the mornings, but they live close to the station, so one hasn't got to take a cab.

LUDOVIC: Perhaps it won't be convenient for them to have you at a moment's notice?

AGATHA: It's not at all convenient for me to go there, but at a time like this one can't stop to think of convenience – especially other people's.

(*Enter* SPARROWBY *cautiously, door left.*)

SPARROWBY: I've been afraid to come in before for fear of meeting Hortensia. I'm awfully hungry; I suppose everything's cold?

LUDOVIC: As a matter of public convenience I request you to be sparing with the ham; it may be required later in the day for an emergency ration of sandwiches. Have you booked a seat in the wagonette?

SPARROWBY: I say, is it as bad as all that? I hoped Mrs Bavvel might have cooled down a bit.

LUDOVIC: She has. She has settled comfortably into a glacial epoch which will transform Briony into a subarctic zone in which I, for one, am not tempted to remain.

SPARROWBY (*seating himself at table and beginning to eat*): What an awful nuisance; I don't at all want to leave Briony just now. I say, do you think I'm engaged to Sybil or not? She certainly seemed to say that we were engaged last night.

LUDOVIC: I really haven't given it a thought. I don't think it matters particularly. The important question is, is Trevor engaged to anybody?

SPARROWBY: I think you're awfully unsympathetic.

LUDOVIC: It's absurd to expect sympathy at breakfast time. Breakfast is the most unsympathetic meal of the day. One can't love one's neighbour with any sincerity when he's emptying the toast rack and helping himself lavishly to the grilled mushrooms that one particularly adores. Even at lunch one is usually in rather a quarrelsome frame of mind; you must have noticed that most family rows take place at lunchtime. At afternoon tea one begins to get polite, but one isn't really sympathetic till about the second course at dinner.

SPARROWBY: But the whole future happiness of my life is wrapped up in Sybil's acceptance of my offer.

LUDOVIC: People who wrap up their whole future happiness in one event generally find it convenient to unwrap it later on.

(*Enter* CLARE, *door left.*)

CLARE: Morning, everybody. Have you brave things breakfasted with Hortensia?

AGATHA: No, only Ludovic. He reports her as being pretty bad. It's a regular case of *sauve qui peut.**

CLARE: Such disgusting weather to travel in. Fancy being cooped up in a stuffy railway carriage all the afternoon. Anything in the papers, Ludovic?

LUDOVIC: Very possibly there may be. Agatha and Sparrowby have kept me so pleasantly engaged in discussing their plans that I've scarcely been able to grapple with the wider events of the day.

AGATHA: Oh, I can always read and carry on a conversation at the same time. I suppose I've got a double brain.

CLARE: Why don't you economise and have one good one?

LUDOVIC (*rising*): If you two are going to quarrel, I'm off. Other people's quarrels always make me feel amiable, and a prospective Parliamentary candidate can't afford to be amiable in private life. It's like talking shop out of hours. (*Walks towards door left.*)

SPARROWBY (*jumping up and following him*): I say, Ludovic, I want to ask you – do you really think—

(*Exeunt* LUDOVIC *and* SPARROWBY, *door left. Enter* MRS VULPY, *door centre.*)

MRS VULPY: Is the coast clear? I'm scared to death of meeting that gorgon* again.

AGATHA: Had breakfast?

MRS VULPY: Nothing worth speaking of. Oh, is there tea? How adorable. (*Seats herself at table.*) Well, has anything happened?

AGATHA: The luggage cart has been requisitioned, and if you want anything in the way of sandwiches or luggage labels an early order will prevent disappointment.

MRS VULPY: Gracious, what an earthquake. And all because of a little harmless dance. If any of you girls do succeed in marrying that young man, you'll have to break him of the farmyard habit. A husband who is always going to earth is rather a poor sort of investment.

CLARE: As long as one marries him, what *does* it matter? One can afford to be neglected by one's own husband; it's when other people's husbands neglect one that one begins to talk of matrimonial disillusion.

MRS VULPY: Other people's husbands are rather an over-rated lot. I prefer unmarried men any day; they've so much more experience.

CLARE: I don't agree with you. Isn't there a proverb: 'A relapsed husband makes the best rake'?*

AGATHA: You're positively disgraceful, both of you. We used to be taught to be content with the Ten Commandments and one husband; nowadays women get along with fewer commandments and want ten husbands.

MRS VULPY: It's no use scolding. It's the fault of the age we live in. The perfection of the motor car has turned the country into a vast prairie of grass-widowhood.* How can a woman be expected to cleave to someone who's

at Lancaster Gate one minute and at North Berwick the
next?

AGATHA: She can stay at home and lavish her affections on
her babies.

CLARE: I hate babies. They're so human – they remind one
of monkeys.

(*Enter* SYBIL, *door left; throws herself into chair left centre of stage.*)

MRS VULPY: Well, it's no use taking a tragic view of
yesterday's fiasco. There are thousands of as good men
as Trevor in the world, waiting to be married.

SYBIL: That's just it – they don't seem to mind how long they
wait. And when you come to have a closer look at the
thousands, there are very few of them that one could
possibly marry.

AGATHA: Oh, nonsense; I don't see why one should be so
dreadfully fastidious. After all, we're told all men are
brothers.

SYBIL: Yes; unfortunately, so many of them are younger
brothers.

AGATHA: Oh, well, money isn't everything.

SYBIL: It isn't everything, but it's a very effective substitute
for most things.

MRS VULPY: By the way, tell me which is the nearest and
cleanest way to the farm.

AGATHA (*who is about to leave room*): Through the white
gates into the fir plantation, and past the potting sheds.
You can't miss it. (*Suddenly turning back and sitting down
abruptly.*) What do you want to go there for?

MRS VULPY: Merely to say my goodbyes to Mr Trevor, and while he is showing me round the farm buildings I dare say I'll find an opportunity to tell him how badly he's treated you all, and what an uncomfortable situation he's created, and generally work on his better feelings.

SYBIL: You might as well work on superior blotting paper.

(*Exit* MRS VULPY.)

I don't trust that woman a little atom.

CLARE: I believe she's had bad news from South Africa, and she's keeping it dark and going for Trevor on her own account.

SYBIL: He spoke very curiously about her to me last night – asked what I thought of her and all that.

AGATHA: Exactly what he did to me. I say, can't we stop her?

CLARE: Are you proposing to use violence? If so I think I'll watch from a distance; when you used to play hockey you were noted for hitting more people than you ever aimed at.

SYBIL (*jumping to her feet*): Hortensia's voice!

(CLARE *and* SYBIL *scurry out of the room by door right.* AGATHA *blunders into the arms of* HORTENSIA, *who enters by door left.*)

AGATHA (*trying to look at her ease*): Oh, good morning. Did it rain in the night?

HORTENSIA: I lay awake most of the night; I did not hear any rain. (*Rings bell.*)

139

AGATHA: Oh, I'm *so* sorry you didn't sleep well. Oak leaves
 soaked in saltwater and put under the bed are an awfully
 good remedy. Let me get you some.

HORTENSIA (*coldly*): Thank you, we don't want any more
 decaying vegetation brought into the house. My
 sleeplessness was not due to insomnia. Under normal
 circumstances I sleep excellently.

AGATHA: I feel that I ought to explain about last night.

HORTENSIA: You will have to explain. Everyone will have
 to give an account of his or her share in the disgraceful
 affair, including the servants, who seem to have con-
 nived at it. I have ordered a gathering of the household for 4 o'clock in the library, which you will kindly
 attend.

(*Enter* WILLIAM, *door centre.*)

William, at this hour of the morning I expect the breakfast things to be cleared away. (*Exit, right.*)

AGATHA: William, tell John that I shall have to leave here well
 before four to catch the 4.15. I've got lots of luggage to
 register at the station.

WILLIAM: Yes, miss; the wagonette's ordered already.

AGATHA: I expect it will have to be the dogcart as well; there
 will probably be a lot of us wanting to catch trains this
 afternoon.

WILLIAM: Yes, miss. What I envy about you, miss, is your
 play-going way of taking things.

AGATHA: Play-going way?

WILLIAM: Yes, miss. You just sit and wait till things has been
 brought to a climax, and then you put on your hat and

140

gloves and walk outside. It's different for those who've got to go on living with the climax.

AGATHA: I hadn't thought of that; I suppose it is rather horrid.

(*Exit* WILLIAM *by door centre, carrying off breakfast things on tray. Exit* AGATHA, *door left. Enter* LUDOVIC, *door right. He takes newspaper packet off table left, opens wrapper, throws himself into a chair and begins reading. Enter* RENÉ, *door right.*)

RENÉ: Ludovic! Aren't you all feeling like a lot of drowned kittens?

LUDOVIC: I don't know what a lot of drowned kittens feel like. I hope I'm not looking like a lot of drowned kittens.

RENÉ: Oh, don't talk about looks. (*Looks himself carefully over in the mirror.*) I felt so jumpy last night that I scarcely dared put the light out. I had a hot-water bottle in my bed.

LUDOVIC: A hot-water bottle? Surely it's too warm for that?

RENÉ: Oh, there was no hot water in it, it was merely to give a sense of protection. I suppose there's a general stampede? (*Seats himself, chair centre stage.*)

LUDOVIC: The house resounds with the cutting of sandwiches and the writing of luggage labels.

RENÉ: And what does *he* say to it all?

LUDOVIC: Who? Trevor? He made a strategic move to the farm at an early hour.

RENÉ: I believe he was so sleepy last night that he doesn't really know whether he proposed to Sybil or not.

LUDOVIC: Sybil did her best, but that miserable Sparrowby ruined whatever chance she had.

RENÉ: I've no use for that person; he's just the kind of idiot who comes up to you in a Turkish bath and says, 'Isn't it hot?' Meanwhile, what are you going to do?

LUDOVIC: I shall pay a long-projected visit to an old chum who lives in Kildare.

RENÉ: Nonsense, Ludo, you can't. Nobody really lives in Kildare; I don't believe there are such places. And old Spindleham is really at the last gasp. The *Western Morning News* says he can't live out the week.

LUDOVIC: Under present circumstances, René, I've no intention of standing.

RENÉ: Oh, don't be so provoking. Go and see Trevor and tell him he must marry Sybil. Explain the circumstances to him. A wife is a sort of thing that can happen any day. But a Parliamentary vacancy is a different matter. There's your career to think of.

LUDOVIC: He will naturally retort that his whole future happiness has got to be thought of.

RENÉ: Oh, damn! What about my whole future income?

LUDOVIC: My dear René, the question is whether we have not hunted Trevor into the wrong net. I have just met that Vulpy woman in full cry up to the farm, and something in her manner tells me that she's running a trail of her own.

RENÉ: But her husband—

LUDOVIC: I asked her if she had had any news of him. She was careful to tell me that she hadn't received any letters this morning. She was equally careful *not* to inform me that she did get a telegram. I fancy that telegram announced her promotion to the rank of widowhood.

RENÉ: But you surely don't think that Trevor would—

LUDOVIC: That's exactly what I do think. We've tried to badger and harry him into a matrimonial entanglement with all sorts of eligible and likely young women, and it's quite in the nature of things that he'll turn round and perversely commit himself to this wholly impossible person. You must remember that Trevor is a fellow who has seen comparatively little of the world, and what he's seen has been more or less of one pattern. Now that he's suddenly confronted with a creature of quite another type, with whom he isn't expected to interest himself, naturally he at once becomes interested.

RENÉ: Well, if this stumbling block of a husband of hers has really been good-natured enough to migrate to another world, everything is plain sailing. Trevor can go ahead and marry the lady – after a decent interval, of course.

LUDOVIC: Absolutely out of the question. I should never forgive myself if such a thing happened.

RENÉ: But why – haven't we been moving heaven and earth to get him married?

LUDOVIC: Married, yes, but not to Mrs Vulpy. After all, Trevor is my only brother's only son, and if I can help it I'm not going to sit still and let him tie himself to that bundle of scheming vulgarity. Besides, a woman like that installed as mistress of Briony would only mean a prolongation of Hortensia's influence. Trevor would be driven to consult his mother in everything, from the sheer impossibility of putting confidence in his wife.

143

RENÉ: I think we're being absurdly fastidious about Trevor's wife. We've given him heaps of opportunities for marrying decent nonentities, so I don't see why we should reproach ourselves if he accidentally swallows a clumsier bait. Anyhow, I don't see how you're going to stop it if there's really anything in it.

LUDOVIC: That's just what's worrying me. To speak to him about it would be to clinch matters. With rare exceptions the Bavvels are devilishly obstinate.

RENÉ: Well, it would be rather a delicate subject to broach to her. She would scarcely relish being told that she's impossible.

LUDOVIC: I should put it more tactfully. I should tell her she wouldn't harmonise with local surroundings, that she has too much dash and go and... help me out with some tactful attribute.

RENÉ: Too flamboyant.

LUDOVIC: I asked you for tact, not truth.

RENÉ: Too much individuality? I don't know what that means. But it sounds well.

LUDOVIC: Thank you, that will do nicely. A woman always respects a word that she can't spell.

RENÉ: You'd better jot it all down on your cuff. You'll forget it in a sudden panic when you're talking to her.

(*Enter* BUTLER, *right.*)

BUTLER: Colonel Mutsome.

(*Enter* COLONEL MUTSOME, *right. Exit* BUTLER, *same door.*)

144

COLONEL MUTSOME: How do you do? (*Shakes hands with* LUDOVIC, *bows to* RENÉ.) What unpleasant weather. Quite damp. I hope dear Hortensia is well? I've a great admiration for Hortensia. I always say she's the first lady in Somersetshire.

RENÉ: Everything must have a beginning.

COLONEL MUTSOME: I hear our Member is not expected to live. (*Seats himself in chair, right.*)

LUDOVIC: I saw something to that effect in the local papers.

COLONEL MUTSOME: I suppose we shall be having an election in a few weeks' time. Is it true that you are the prospective party candidate?

LUDOVIC: I saw it suggested in the local papers. There has always been some idea of getting a Bavvel to stand.

COLONEL MUTSOME: I suppose you would accept?

LUDOVIC: That will depend very largely on family considerations.

RENÉ: Of course Ludovic means to stand. I caught him yesterday being ostentatiously sympathetic to the local chemist, a man with a harelip* and personal reminiscences and a vote. No one listens to the personal reminiscences of a man with a harelip unless they've got some imperative motive; when the man also has a vote the motive is unmistakable.

LUDOVIC: René, as a private secretary, you would have to be very private.

COLONEL MUTSOME: I suppose you subscribe to all the principal items of the party programme?

LUDOVIC: Oh, I believe so – and to most of the local charities. That is the really important thing. It is generally understood that a rich man has some difficulty in entering the Kingdom of Heaven; the House of Commons is not so exclusive. Our electoral system, however, takes good care that the rich man entering Parliament shall not remain rich. It is simply astonishing the number of institutions supported by involuntary contributions that a candidate discovers in his prospective constituency. At least, he doesn't discover them — they discover him. For instance, I don't keep bees — I don't know how to, and don't want to know how to. I don't eat honey. I never go near a hive except at an agricultural show, when I am perfectly certain there are no bees in it. Yet I have already consented to be vice president and annual subscriber to the local beekeepers' association. On consulting a memorandum book I find I am vice president of seven bell-ringers' guilds and about twenty village football clubs. I cannot remember having been so enthusiastic about football when I was at school. I am a subscribing member of a botanical ramble club. Can you imagine me doing botanical rambles? Of course, you quite understand that there's no bribery in all this.

COLONEL MUTSOME: Oh, of course not. Bribery is not tolerated nowadays.

LUDOVIC: At any rate, one gives it another name. Let us call it altruism in compartments; very intense and comprehensive where it exists, but strictly confined within the bound of one's constituency.

COLONEL MUTSOME: I suppose you're sound on religious questions? There is no truth in the story that you have leanings towards agnosticism?

LUDOVIC: My dear Colonel, no one can be agnostic nowadays. The Christian Apologists* have left one nothing to disbelieve.

RENÉ: Personally I am a pagan. Christians waste too much time in professing to be miserable sinners, which generally results in their being merely miserable and leaving some of the best sins undone; whereas the pagan gets cheerfully to work and commits his sins and doesn't brag so much about them.

COLONEL MUTSOME: I trust you are only talking in theory?

RENÉ: In theory, of course. In practice, everyone is pagan according to his lights.

LUDOVIC: René, as a private secretary, I'm afraid you would become a public scandal. I shouldn't dare to leave you alone with an unprotected deputation.

(*Enter* TREVOR, *door left.*)

TREVOR: Morning, Ludovic. Hullo, Colonel, I didn't know you were here. (*Shakes hands with* COLONEL MUTSOME.) Morning, René. I distinctly heard you all talking politics. (*Seats himself in chair, centre stage.*)

COLONEL MUTSOME: Politics are rather in the air. It seems we are threatened with a Parliamentary vacancy.

LUDOVIC: By way of meeting trouble halfway, Colonel Mutsome has come to ascertain whether there is any probability of my standing.

COLONEL MUTSOME: I should have expressed it differently.

LUDOVIC: Things do not point at present to the probability of my becoming a candidate, but the Colonel has taken things betimes* and has been doing a little preliminary heckling.

COLONEL MUTSOME: Not heckling, exactly. My position as vice chairman of the local party association gives me some opportunity for gauging opinion down here. Collectively the Government has, perhaps, lost some of its prestige, but individually I think ministers are popular.

LUDOVIC: Including the irrepressible Bumpingford.

COLONEL MUTSOME: Oh, certainly. Rather an assertive personality, perhaps, but of undeniable ability. He comes into the category of those who are born to command.

LUDOVIC: Possibly. His trouble so far is that he hasn't been able to find anyone who was born to obey him. So you think ministers are in general popular?

COLONEL MUTSOME: Compared with the leaders of the opposition—

LUDOVIC: One should be careful not to say disparaging things of opposition leaders.

COLONEL MUTSOME: Because they may one day be at the head of affairs?

LUDOVIC: No, because they may one day lead the opposition. One never knows.

COLONEL MUTSOME: There is the question of votes for women.

LUDOVIC: Personally I see no reason why women shouldn't have votes. They're quite unfit to have votes, but that's no argument against their having them. If we were to restrict the right of voting to those of the male sex who were fitted for it we should have to enlarge Hyde Park to accommodate the protesting hordes of non-voters. Government by democracy means government of the mentally unfit by the mentally mediocre tempered by the saving grace of snobbery.

COLONEL MUTSOME: You will be very unpopular if you say that sort of thing down here.

LUDOVIC: I have no intention of saying it. Some poet has remarked, 'To think is to be full of sorrow.'* To think aloud is a luxury of sorrow which few politicians can afford to indulge in.

COLONEL MUTSOME (*suddenly*): By the way, was there some dancing at Briony last night?

LUDOVIC (*in nervous haste*): Oh, no, just some Shakespeare readings and a little music. I wonder you haven't asked me about land values.

COLONEL MUTSOME: I was coming to that.

TREVOR (*eagerly*): It's rather an important question, particularly down here.

LUDOVIC: Most important.

RENÉ (*same eagerness*): It's quite one of the questions of the immediate future. An aunt of a cabinet minister was speaking to me about it only last week. She said it kept her awake at nights.

COLONEL MUTSOME: Really — I quite understood that there was a Cinderella dance—

LUDOVIC: Oh, no, dear no, nothing of that kind. Some Shakespeare reading, in costume.

COLONEL MUTSOME: In costume? But how very interesting. What scenes did you give?

RENÉ: The ghost scenes from what-do-you-call-it.

COLONEL MUTSOME: The ghost scene from *Hamlet*?* That must have needed a lot of rehearsal.

RENÉ: No, we had a lot of ghosts, so that if one forgot his lines another could go on with them.

COLONEL MUTSOME: What an odd idea. What a very odd idea. But they couldn't all have been in costume.

RENÉ: They were — rows of them. All in white sheets.

COLONEL MUTSOME: How very extraordinary. It couldn't have been a bit like Shakespeare.

RENÉ: It wasn't, but it was very like Maeterlinck.* Whoever really wrote *Hamlet*, there can be no doubt that Maeterlinck and Maxim Gorky* ought to have written it in collaboration.

COLONEL MUTSOME: But how could they? They weren't born at that time.

RENÉ: That's the bother of it. Ideas get used up so quickly. If the Almighty hadn't created the world at the beginning of things Edison would probably have done it by this time on quite different lines, and then someone would have come along to prove that the Chinese had done it centuries ago.

COLONEL MUTSOME (*acidly, to* TREVOR, *turning his back on* RENÉ): How is your cold, Mr Trevor? You had a cold before we went to Worcestershire.

TREVOR: That one went long ago. I've got another one now, which is better, thank you.

COLONEL MUTSOME: We had such a lot of asparagus in Worcestershire.

TREVOR: Yes?

COLONEL MUTSOME: We got our earliest asparagus in London, then we got more down here, and then we had a late edition in Worcestershire, so we've had quite a lot this year.

RENÉ: The charm of that story is that it could be told in any drawing room.

COLONEL MUTSOME (*rising from seat*): I think I saw Hortensia pass the window. If you don't mind I'll go and meet her.

LUDOVIC: Let me escort you.

(*Exeunt* LUDOVIC *and* COLONEL MUTSOME, *door right.*)

RENÉ (*lighting cigarette*): You've heard the story that's going about?

TREVOR: That we held unholy revels here last night?

RENÉ: Well, apropos of that, people are saying that you and Sparrowby proposed to the same girl and that Sparrowby threatened to break your neck if you didn't give way to him, and that you gave way rather than have any unpleasantness.

TREVOR: What an infernal invention. I am damned if I let that go about.

RENÉ: I don't see what you can do to stop it.

TREVOR: I might break Sparrowby's neck.

RENÉ: No one could have any reasonable objection to that course – Sparrowby is one of those people who would be enormously improved by death. Unfortunately, he is your guest, and on that account it wouldn't be quite the thing to do. He's sure to have a parent or aunt or someone who'd write letters to *The Times* about it – 'Fatal ragging in country houses,' and so on. No, your only prudent line of action would be to marry the girl, or any girl who came handy, just to knock the stuffing out of the story. Otherwise you'll have to take it recumbent, as the saying is.

TREVOR: I'm not fool enough to rush off and perpetrate matrimony with the first person I meet in order to put a stop to a ridiculous story.

RENÉ: My dear Trevor, I quite understand your situation.

TREVOR: You don't.

RENÉ: Of course I do. You don't want to interrupt an agreeable and moderately safe flirtation with a woman who
has just got husband enough to give her the flavour of
forbidden fruit. I'm not one of those who run the Vulpy
down just because she's a trifle too flamboyant for the
general taste. As a wife I dare say she'd be rather an
experiment down here, but I've no doubt you'd be toler-
ably happy. She'd be more at her ease at a suburban race
meeting than at a county garden party, but still — you
could travel a good deal. And if you find her sympathetic
it doesn't matter so very much whether she's intelligent
or not. But all that is beside the point, because she's not
available. Inconvenient husbands don't come to timely
ends in real life like they do in fiction. If you seriously
want to put your foot down on the gossip that is going
about, and make an end of this uncomfortable domestic
situation, your only course is to go straight ahead and
propose to the first available girl that you run up against.
If it's the bother of the thing that you shirk, let me open
negotiations for you — my mission in life is to save other
people trouble, on reasonable terms. (*Becomes suddenly
aware that* TREVOR *has gone to sleep, and rises angrily from
his seat.*) Of all the exasperating dolts! I don't know how
matchmaking mothers manage to grow fat on the business; a week of this would wear me to a shadow.

(*Exit* RENÉ *in a fury, door right. Enter* LUDOVIC, *left.*)

LUDOVIC: Hullo, is René here?
TREVOR: He was a minute or two ago. I think I heard him
leave the house.

LUDOVIC: Has anything been heard of his mother? So many distracting things have been happening that I clean forgot to ask about her.

TREVOR: By Jove, so did I. He'll think us rather remiss, but anyhow, he seemed more concerned about finding me a suitable wife than about retrieving his lost parent. Have you heard anything of the story that he says is going about?

LUDOVIC (*seating himself*): About last night, you mean?

TREVOR: Yes, that Sparrowby and I proposed to the same girl, and that Sparrowby bounced me into taking a back seat.

LUDOVIC: Ah! No – at least, probably what I heard had reference to that. What an unpleasant scandal. Unfortunately, the fact that Sybil is leaving Briony in such a hurry will give colour to it.

TREVOR: Was it Sybil, then?

LUDOVIC: I suppose so. I think I heard her name mentioned. What shall you do then?

TREVOR: Do? I don't know. What do you suggest?

LUDOVIC: My suggestion would be so simple that you are not likely to accept it for a moment. If one shows people an intricate and risky way out of a difficulty they are becomingly grateful: if you point out a safe and obvious exit they regard you with resentment. In your case the resentment would probably take the form of going to sleep in the middle of my advice.

TREVOR: I wasn't going to sleep! I was wondering which particular girl you were going to recommend to my notice. There seems to be a concentration on Sybil Bomont.

LUDOVIC: It's scarcely my place to fill in the details for you;
I suppose matrimony is an eventuality which begins
to present itself rather prominently to you, and when
you've settled that point the details soon fit themselves
in. If the Bomont girl doesn't meet with your require-
ments there is your neighbour Evelyn Bray, whom you
entangled in last night's entertainment – I shall never
forget her face when I told her that Hortensia didn't
require any more music – and there's Clare Henessey;
you used to get on famously with Clare.

TREVOR: Clare and Evelyn are very good sorts—

LUDOVIC (*raising his hand*): Good sorts? Oh, my dear Trevor,
you are still in the schoolboy stage as regards women.
The schoolboy divides womenkind broadly into two
species – the decent sort and the holy horror – much
as the naturalist, after a somewhat closer investigation
of his subject, classifies snakes as either harmless or
poisonous. The schoolboy is usually fairly well informed
about things that he doesn't have to study, but as regards
women he is altogether too specific. You can't really
divide them in a hard-and-fast way.

TREVOR: At least there are superficial differences.

LUDOVIC: But nothing deeper. Woman is a belated sur-
vival from a primeval age of struggle and cunning and
competition; that is why, wherever you go, the world
over, you find all the superfluous dust and worry being
made by the gentler sex. If you are on a crowded
P. & O. steamer,* who is it that wages an incessant
warfare over the cabin accommodation? Who is it
that creates the little social feuds that divide benighted
country parishes and lonely hill stations? Who is it

that raises objections to smoking in railway carriages, and who writes to housemasters to complain of the dear boys' breakfast fare? Man has moved with the historic progression of the ages, but woman is a habit that has survived from the period when one had to dispute with cave bears and cave hyenas whether one ate one's supper or watched others eat it, whether one slept at home or on one's doorstep. The great religions of the world have all recognised this fact and kept womankind severely outside of their respective systems. That is why, however secular one's tendencies, one turns instinctively to religion in some form for respite and peace.

TREVOR: But one can't get along without women.

LUDOVIC: Precisely what I have been trying to impress upon you. Granted that woman is merely a bad habit, she is a habit that we have not grown out of. Under certain circumstances a bad habit is first cousin to a virtue. In your case it seems to me that matrimony is not only a virtue but a convenience.

TREVOR: It's all very well for you to talk about convenience. What may be convenient for other people may be highly inconvenient for me.

LUDOVIC: That means that you're involved in some blind-alley affair with a married woman. Precisely what I feared. Men like yourself of easy-going, unsuspecting temperament invariably fall victims to the most rapacious type of cave woman, the woman who already has a husband and who merely kills for the sake of killing. You pick and choose and dally among your artificial categories of awfully good sorts and dear little women, and then someone of the Mrs Vulpy type comes along and quietly annexes you.

TREVOR: I seem to have been annexed to Mrs Vulpy by popular delimitation. Critically speaking, she isn't a bit my style, but I don't see anything so very dreadful about her. She's a trifle pronounced, perhaps – she tells me she had a Spanish grandfather.

LUDOVIC: Ancestors will happen in the best-intentioned families. Every social sin or failing is excused nowadays under the plea of an artistic temperament or a Sicilian grandmother. As poor Lady Cloutsham once told me, as soon as her children found out that a Hungarian lady of blameless moral character had married into the family somewhere in the reign of the Georges,* they considered themselves absolved from any further attempts to distinguish between good and evil – except by way of expressing a general preference for the latter. When her youngest boy was at Winchester he made such unblushing use of the Hungarian strain in his blood that he was known as the Blue Danube.* 'That,' said Lady Cloutsham, 'is what comes of letting young children read Debrett* and Darwin.'

TREVOR: As regards Mrs Vulpy's temperament, I don't fancy one need go very far afield.

LUDOVIC: Oh, no, Greater London is quite capable of turning her out without having recourse to foreign blending.

TREVOR: Still, I don't see that she's anything worse than a flirt.

LUDOVIC: Oh, on her best behaviour, I've no doubt she's perfectly gentle and frolicsome; for the matter of that, the cave hyenas probably had their after-dinner moments of comparative amiability. But, from the point of view of an extremely marriageable young bachelor, she simply isn't safe to play with. I don't want to run her down on the score of her rather common personality, but I wish to warn you that she is one of those people gifted with just the sort of pushing, scheming audacity—

(*Enter* MRS VULPY, *door centre.*)

Ah, good morning, Mrs Vulpy.

(TREVOR *looks round and jumps to his feet.*)

Just the sort of pushing, scheming audacity that makes them dangerous. Once we let them wriggle their way into the Persian Gulf they'll snap up all our commerce under our eyes.

MRS VULPY: You dreadful men, always talking politics.

LUDOVIC: Politics are rather in the air just now.

MRS VULPY: I feel as if we were all in the air after the dreadful explosion of last night. I am just wondering where I am going to come down.

TREVOR: It seems an awful shame, driving all you charming people away. My mother goes to absurd lengths about some things.

MRS VULPY: It's poor us who have to go the absurd lengths. I shan't feel safe till I have put two fair-sized counties between Mrs Bavvel and myself. Oh, Mr Trevor, before I leave you *must* show me the model dairy.

TREVOR: Right-oh. I'll take you there now, if you like.

MRS VULPY: Do, please. I just love dairies and cheese-making and all that sort of thing. I think it's so clever the way they make those little blue insertions in Gorgonzola cheese. I always say I ought to have been a farmer's wife. We'll leave Ludovic to his horrid politics.

LUDOVIC: Before I forget, Trevor, go and get me those trout flies you promised me, and I'll have them packed. Mrs Vulpy won't mind, I dare say, waiting for you here for a few minutes.

TREVOR: Right you are. I won't be a second. (*Exit.*)

LUDOVIC: I hope you don't despise me too much.

MRS VULPY: Despise you! Oh, Mr Ludovic, what ever should I despise you for?

LUDOVIC: For being fool enough to put confidence in you as a fellow conspirator.

MRS VULPY: Why, I am sure I have been loyal enough to our compact. If the results haven't been brilliant, you can scarcely blame me for the breakdown.

LUDOVIC: The compact was that you should help in an endeavour to get Trevor engaged to one of the girls of the house party. I don't think I'm mistaken in saying that the game you are playing is to secure him for yourself.

MRS VULPY: Never more mistaken in your life. Really, you seem to forget that I'm a married woman.

LUDOVIC: Your memory is even shorter. You seem to forget that you received a telegram this morning to say that your husband is dead.

MRS VULPY: Whatever will you say next? You don't know what you're talking about.

LUDOVIC: Oh, it's correct enough; I read it.

MRS VULPY (*raising her voice*): How dare you intercept my correspondence! The telegram was marked plain enough – 'Vulpy, c/o Bavvel.' You're simply a common sneak.

LUDOVIC: I didn't read the intelligence in your telegram. I read it in your manner. You've just been obliging enough to confirm my deductions.

MRS VULPY: Oh, you're trying amateur detective business on me, are you? (*With sudden change of manner:*) Now, look here, Mr Ludovic, don't you set yourself against me. Why shouldn't I marry Trevor? You said yourself two days ago that it was a pity I wasn't a widow, so that I could be eligible for marrying him.

LUDOVIC: Of course, I spoke jestingly.

MRS VULPY: Well, it isn't a jest to me. I have had a wretched, miserable time with my late husband; I can't tell you what a time I've had with him.

LUDOVIC: Because you have had a miserable time with the late Mr Vulpy is precisely, my dear lady, the reason why I don't wish you to try the experiment of being miserable with my nephew. You are so utterly unsuited to him and his surroundings that you couldn't fail to be unhappy and to make him unhappy into the bargain.

MRS VULPY: I don't see why I should be unsuited to him. Trevor is a gentleman, and I am a lady, I suppose. Perhaps you wish to suggest that I am not.

LUDOVIC: You are – if you will permit me to say so – a very charming and agreeable lady, but you would not fit in with the accepted ideals of the neighbourhood. You have too much dash and go and... in... indefinable... characteristics. I don't know if you've noticed it, but in Somersetshire we don't dash.

MRS VULPY: Oh, don't fling your beastly county set and its prejudices in my face. I am as good as the lot of you, and a bit better. I mix in far smarter circles than you've got here. Lulu Duchess of Dulverton and her set are a cut above the pack of you, and as for you, if you want my opinion, you're a meddling, interfering, middle-aged toad.

LUDOVIC: You asked me a moment ago why you shouldn't marry Trevor. You're supplying one of the reasons now. You're flying into something very like a rage. In Somersetshire we never fly into a rage. We walk into one, and when necessary we stay there for weeks, perhaps for years. But we never fly into one.

MRS VULPY: Oh, I've had enough of your sarcasms. You've had my opinion of you. You're a mass of self-seeking and intrigue. You're mistaken if you think I'm going to let a middle-aged toad stand in my path.

(*Enter* TREVOR.)

TREVOR: Here are all the flies I could find. Sorry to have kept you waiting, but I had to hunt for them.

LUDOVIC: Don't mention it – we've been having such an interesting talk about the age toads live to. Mrs Vulpy is quite a naturalist.

MRS VULPY: I've got all my packing to do, so we'd better not lose any more time.

TREVOR: Right you are; we will go at once.

(*Exeunt* TREVOR *and* MRS VULPY, *right. Enter* AGATHA, *left.* LUDOVIC *flings himself down savagely at writing table.*)

AGATHA: Have you seen Trevor anywhere?

LUDOVIC: He was here a minute ago. I believe he's now in the dairy.

AGATHA: The dairy! What's he doing in the dairy?

LUDOVIC: I don't know. What does one do in dairies?

AGATHA: One makes butter and that sort of thing. Trevor can't make butter.

LUDOVIC: I don't believe he can. We spend incredible sums on technical education, but the number of people who know how to make butter remains extremely limited.

AGATHA: Is he alone?

LUDOVIC: I fancy Mrs Vulpy is with him.

AGATHA: That cat! Why is she with him?

LUDOVIC: I don't know. There's a proverb, isn't there? About showing a cat the way to the dairy, but I forget what happens next.*

AGATHA: I call it rather compromising.

LUDOVIC: It's a model dairy, you know.

AGATHA: I don't see that that makes it any better. Mrs Vulpy is scarcely a model woman.

LUDOVIC: She's a married woman.

AGATHA: A South African husband is rather a doubtful security.

LUDOVIC: Then you can scarcely blame her for taking a provident interest in West of England bachelors.

AGATHA: It's simply indecent. She might wait till one husband is definitely dead before trying to rope in another.

LUDOVIC: My dear Agatha, brevity is the soul of widowhood.

AGATHA: I loathe her. She promised she would try to get Trevor to put an end to all this muddle and row by getting him engaged to... to Sybil, or anyone else available.

LUDOVIC: How do you know she's not trying now?

AGATHA: Oh, I say, do you think she is?

LUDOVIC: I think it's quite possible; also I think it's quite possible that Trevor is discoursing learnedly on the amount of milk a Jersey cow can be induced to yield under intelligent treatment. Frankly, I consider these milk and egg statistics that one is expected to talk about in the country to border on the indelicate. If I were a cow or hen I should resent having my most private and personal actions treated as a sort of auction bridge. The country has no reticence.

(*Enter* SYBIL, *right.*)

SYBIL: Well, I've packed.

AGATHA: Oh dear, I haven't begun. I know I shall be late for the train; I'm always late for trains. I must go and dig up some foxglove roots in the plantation to take away with me.

SYBIL: I refuse to let you bring more than five cubic feet of earth mould and stinging nettles into the carriage.

AGATHA: Don't excite yourself, my dear. I'm going by a down train and you're going by an up, I presume.

SYBIL: Don't be a pig. You must come with us to make a four for bridge; there'll be Clare and myself and you and the Vulpy. Otherwise we'll have to let that wearisome Sparrowby in, and I'd rather have a ton of decaying hedge and compressed caterpillar in the carriage than have Sparrowby inflicted on me for three mortal hours.

AGATHA: I'm not going to upset all my visiting plans just to suit your bridge arrangements. Besides, you said the last time we played that I had no more notion of the game than an unborn parrot. I haven't got such a short memory, you see.

SYBIL: I wish you hadn't got such a short temper.

AGATHA: Me, short-tempered? My good temper is proverbial!

SYBIL: Not to say legendary.

LUDOVIC: Please don't start quarrelling. You're making me feel amiable again.

(*Enter* MRS VULPY, *right, trying not to look crest-fallen.*)

MRS VULPY: I never knew a dairy could be so interesting. All the latest improvements. Such beautiful ventilation – and such plain dairymaids. What it is to have a careful mother.

LUDOVIC: You weren't very long in going over it.

MRS VULPY: Oh, I had to rush it, of course. I must go and superintend my packing. It doesn't do to leave everything to one's maid.

SYBIL: Hortensia! It's no use bolting – we're cornered.

(*Enter right* HORTENSIA *and* COLONEL MUTSOME.)

MRS VULPY: Good morning, Mrs Bavvel.

(MRS VULPY *bows to the* COLONEL. *Pause.*)

COLONEL MUTSOME: Mrs Bavvel has just been show-ing me the poultry yard. I've been admiring the black Minorcas.* How many eggs did you say they've laid in the last six months, Hortensia?

HORTENSIA: I don't think Mrs Vulpy is much interested in such matters.

MRS VULPY: Oh, I adore poultry. There's something so Omar Khayyám* about them. Lulu Duchess of Dulverton keeps white peacocks. (*Pause.*)

COLONEL MUTSOME: Such a disappointment to us not to have had Mrs Bavvel's lecture last night. All on account of Mrs St Gall's extraordinary disappearance. People are talking of a suicide. Others say it's a question of eluding creditors. Her debts, I believe, are simply enormous.

HORTENSIA: One must be careful of echoing local gossip, but from the improvident way in which that household is managed one is justified in supposing that financial difficulties are not unknown there.

COLONEL MUTSOME: In any case, I feel convinced that we shan't see Mrs St Gall in these parts again.

(*Enter* RENÉ, *door right, followed by* TREVOR.)

RENÉ: I've found my mother!

COLONEL MUTSOME: Mrs St Gall found? You've seen her?

RENÉ: No, but I've spoken to her. She was having a bath when I got back, so we conversed through the bathroom door. Touching scene of filial piety. Return of the prodigal mother, son weeping over bathroom door handle. We don't run to a fatted calf,* but I promised her she should have an egg with her tea.

COLONEL MUTSOME: But where had she been all this time?

RENÉ: Principally at Cardiff.

COLONEL MUTSOME: Cardiff! Whatever did she want to go to Cardiff for?

RENÉ: She didn't want to go. She was taken.

HORTENSIA: Taken!

RENÉ: She was doing a stroll on the Crowcoombe Road when Freda Tewkesbury and her husband swooped down on her in their road car. They live at Warwick – at least they've got a house and some children there – but since they've gone mad on motoring they spend most of their time on the highway. The poor we have always in our midst, and nowadays the rich may crash into us at any moment.

COLONEL MUTSOME: Your mother wasn't run over?

RENÉ: Oh, no, but Freda took her up for a spin and then insisted on her coming on just as she was for a day or two's visit to Monmouth and Cardiff. Freda is always picking up her friends in that impromptu way; she keeps spare toothbrushes and emergency night things of various sizes on her car. Of course, you can't dress for dinner, but that doesn't matter very fundamentally in Cardiff.

LUDOVIC: But surely your mother might have telegraphed to say what had become of her?

RENÉ: She did, from Monmouth, with long directions about charcoal biscuits for the chows'* suppers, and again from Cardiff to say when she was coming back. Freda gave the wires to her husband to send off, which accounts for their never having reached us. None of the Tewkesburys have any memories. Their father got a knock on the head at Inkerman,* and since then the family have never been able to remember anything. I love borrowing odd sums from Tewkesbury; both of us are so absolutely certain to forget all about it.

HORTENSIA: And it was on account of this madcap freak that last night's function was postponed and my address cancelled.

COLONEL MUTSOME: This promiscuous gadding about in motors is undermining all home life and sense of locality. One scarcely knows nowadays to which county people belong.

HORTENSIA: I trust that Mrs St Gall showed some appreciation of the anxiety and alarm caused by her disappearance?

RENÉ: I don't know. I wasn't in a position to see.

HORTENSIA: Altogether a most extraordinary episode – a fitting sequel to last night's saturnalia.

COLONEL MUTSOME: Saturnalia! At Briony?

HORTENSIA: Advantage was taken of my absence at Panfold last night to indulge in an entertainment which I describe as a saturnalia for fear of giving it a worse name.

LUDOVIC: Perhaps we are judging it a little too seriously. A little dancing—

HORTENSIA: Dancing of a particularly objectionable character, in costumes improvised from bed linen.

COLONEL MUTSOME: Bed linen!

HORTENSIA: To an accompaniment of French songs.

COLONEL MUTSOME: *French* songs! But how horrible. I was told that it was merely Shakespeare readings.

HORTENSIA: I regret to say that some of the servants appear to have lent themselves to the furtherance of this underhand proceeding. Among others it will be my unpleasant duty to ask Cook to find another place; I shall give her a good character as a cook, but I shall be very restrained as to what I say about her trustworthiness.

TREVOR: But, Mother, isn't that being rather extreme? She's an awfully good cook.

HORTENSIA: I put conduct before cookery.

TREVOR: After all, she did nothing more than make two or three supper dishes for us; she couldn't be expected to know that there would be French songs to follow.

HORTENSIA: It was her duty to consult me as to these highly unusual preparations. I had given my customary orders for the kitchen department, and they did not include chicken mayonnaise or *Pêches Melba*. Had she informed me of these unauthorised instructions that she had received, the mischief would have been detected and nipped in the bud.

TREVOR: I think it's scarcely fair that she should be punished for what we did. (*Rises and goes to window, right centre.*)

LUDOVIC: I confess I think it's rather unfortunate that such an eminently satisfactory cook should be singled out for dismissal.

HORTENSIA: Scarcely singled out, Ludovic – two or three of the other servants will also have to go.

COLONEL MUTSOME: One must see that one's orders are respected, mustn't one?

(*Enter* WILLIAM, *left, with card.*)

WILLIAM (*to* LUDOVIC): The reporter of the *Wessex Courier* would like to speak with you, sir.

LUDOVIC: Tell him I am unable to see any pressmen at present.

WILLIAM (*handing card to* LUDOVIC): He's written a question which he would feel obliged if you'd answer, sir.

HORTENSIA: What is the question?

LUDOVIC: He wants to know if I intend standing in the event of a Parliamentary vacancy. (*To* WILLIAM:) You can tell him that I have not the remotest intention of standing.

(RENÉ *groans tragically*.)

WILLIAM: Yes, sir. (*Exit left.*)

HORTENSIA: Really, Ludovic, I think you are rather precipitate in your decisions. Differing though we do on more than one of the secondary questions of the day, I am nevertheless inclined to think that the Briony influence would be considerably augmented by having one of the family as Member for the division. Subject to certain modifications of your political views, I am distinctly anxious to see you representing this district in Parliament. I consider this impending vacancy to be a golden opportunity for you.

LUDOVIC: There are some people whose golden opportunities have a way of going prematurely grey. I am one of those.

COLONEL MUTSOME: I must say we rather counted on having you for a candidate. I think I may voice a very general disappointment.

RENÉ: There are some disappointments that are too deep to be voiced.

(*Enter* WILLIAM, *door centre.*)

WILLIAM: If you please, ma'am.

HORTENSIA: What is it?

WILLIAM: Adolphus has laid an egg.

RENÉ: Oh, improper little bird.

HORTENSIA: An egg! How very extraordinary. In all the years that we've had that bird such a thing has never happened. I must admit that I'm rather astonished. See that she has everything she wants and is not disturbed.

WILLIAM: Yes, ma'am.

(*Exit* WILLIAM, *centre. Enter* CLARE, *right, with telegram in hand.*)

CLARE: My great-aunt, Mrs Packington, died at nine o'clock this morning.

(TREVOR *goes into fit of scarcely suppressed laughter.*)

COLONEL MUTSOME: A great age, was she not?

HORTENSIA: A great age, and for longer than I can remember a great invalid. At any rate, a great consumer of medicines. I suppose her death must be regarded as coming in the natural order of things. At the same time, I scarcely think, Trevor, that it is a subject for unbridled amusement.

TREVOR: I'm awfully sorry, but I couldn't help it. It seemed too... too unexpected to be possible. Please excuse me. (*Goes to window and opens it. The others stare at him.*)

169

CLARE: The fact is, I was Mrs Packington's favourite niece. There were things in her will which I couldn't afford to have altered. On the other hand, as I dare say you know, Mrs Bavvel, she had a very special dislike for you.

HORTENSIA: I am aware of it. We had some differences of opinion during my husband's lifetime.

CLARE: It was a favourite observation of hers that you reminded her of a rattlesnake in dove's plumage.

COLONEL MUTSOME: Oh, but what unjust imagery!

CLARE: She hated Briony and everything connected with it, and I had to keep my visits here a dark secret.

COLONEL MUTSOME: How very embarrassing.

CLARE: Not at all. I like duplicity, when it's well done. But when Trevor asked me to marry him it did become embarrassing.

(All the others start up from their seats. Enter WILLIAM, left; stands listening.)

HORTENSIA: Trevor asked you... to marry him?

CLARE: Two months ago. Mrs Packington wasn't expected to live for another fortnight, but she'd been in that precarious condition, off and on, for five years. At the same time, I couldn't risk letting Trevor slip; he'd have forgotten everything and married someone else in sheer absence of mind.

TREVOR: I don't altogether admit that, you know. A thing of that sort I should have remembered.

CLARE: Anyhow, we married on the quiet.

TREVOR: By special licence. It was rather fun – it felt so like doing wrong.

LUDOVIC: Do you mean to tell us that you are Mrs Trevor Bavvel?

CLARE: Of Briony, in the County of Somerset, at your service.

RENÉ (*shouts*): William!

WILLIAM: Yes, sir.

RENÉ: Has that journalist man gone?

WILLIAM: A minute ago, sir.

RENÉ: Quick, send someone after him. Stop him. Tell him—

LUDOVIC: That in the event of a vacancy—

RENÉ: Mr Ludovic Bavvel—

LUDOVIC: Will place himself at the disposal of the party leaders.

RENÉ: Fly! (*Almost pushes* WILLIAM *out of the door, left.*)

CLARE: And, William, tell John to bring up some bottles of Heidsieck.*

WILLIAM: Yes, miss, ma'am.

SYBIL: You dear old thing, you've taken all our breaths away; I always said you and Trevor ought to make a match of it. (*Kisses her.*)

AGATHA: I shall put up evergreens all over the house. (*Kisses her.*)

HORTENSIA: On a subject of such primary importance as choosing a wife I should have preferred – and certainly expected – to be consulted. As you have *chosen* this rather furtive method of doing things, I don't know that there is anything for me to do beyond offering my congratulations, which in the nature of things must be rather perfunctory. I congratulate you both. I trust that the new mistress of Briony will remember that certain traditions of conduct and decorum have reigned here

171

for a generation. I think, without making undue preten-
sions, that Briony has set an example of decent domestic
life to a very large neighbourhood.

CLARE: My dear Hortensia, I think Briony showed last night
what it could do in the way of outgrowing traditions.
Trevor and I have had plenty of time during the last
two months to think out the main features of the new
regime. We shall keep up the model dairy and the
model pigsties, but we've decided that we won't be a
model couple.

(*Enter* JOHN *with four bottles of fizz.*)

JOHN (*to* CLARE): If you please, madam, will the wagonette
and luggage cart be required as ordered?

CLARE: No, I don't think anyone will be leaving today. I shall
expect you all to prolong your visits in our honour. Oh,
of course, I was forgetting Mrs Vulpy has to go up to
Tattersall's to see about some hunters. Just the dogcart,
then.

HORTENSIA: I shall require the carriage for the 4.15 down.
There is a conference at Exeter which I think I ought
to attend.

JOHN: Very well, madam.

(*Exit* JOHN, *left; exeunt* HORTENSIA *and* COLONEL
MUTSOME, *right.*)

AGATHA (*holding up glass*): You dear things, here's your very
good health, and may you have lots and lots of—
RENÉ: Oh, hush!

AGATHA: I was going to say lots of happiness.

RENÉ: Oh, I was afraid you were going to lecture against race suicide.

LUDOVIC
SYBIL
MRS VULPY
RENÉ
} *(speaking together)*: Mr and Mrs Trevor Bavvel!

(They drink.)

TREVOR: Thank you all, and here's to the success of the future Member for the Division—

CLARE: Coupled with that of his charming secretary.

(LUDOVIC *and* RENÉ *bow. Enter* WILLIAM, *centre, with enormous pile of sandwiches.*)

WILLIAM: Please, Cook thought that as the sandwiches wouldn't be wanted for this afternoon you might like them now. Those with mustard on the right, without on the left, sardine and egg in the middle. And, please, I'm asked to express the general rejoicing in the servants' hall, and Cook says that if marriages are made in heaven the angels will be for putting this one in the window as a specimen of their best work.

CLARE: Thank Cook and all of you very much. *(She whispers to* TREVOR.)

TREVOR: Of course, certainly.

CLARE: And tell John to open some Moselle* in the servants' hall for you all to drink our healths. We're coming in presently to get your congratulations.

173

WILLIAM: Yes, ma'am; thank you, ma'am. (*Turns to go.*)

CLARE: And, William…?

WILLIAM (*turning back*): Yes, ma'am?

CLARE: How much did you win on the sweepstake?

(WILLIAM *turns and flies in confusion.*)

CURTAIN

NOTE ON THE TEXT

The texts of 'The Death Trap', 'Karl-Ludwig's Window' and 'The Watched Pot' in this edition are based on those printed in *The Square Egg and Other Sketches, with Three Plays* (1924), a collection published by Saki's sister Ethel after his death. The text of 'The Miracle Merchant' is based on its first publication, in Samuel French's *One-Act Plays for Stage and Study* (Series Eight, 1934). In some cases, spelling and punctuation have been silently corrected, and stage directions given in abbreviated form have been spelt out to make the text more appealing to the modern reader.

NOTES

22   *Gräfin*: A German title equivalent to Countess.

22   *what the world calls a parvenu*: That is, a self-made man. (The word was associated with the *nouveau riche*.)

26   *Henry III period*: Henry III (1207–72) reigned from 1216 until 1272.

27   *I have killed the Archduke*: This play is perhaps inspired by the assassination of Archduke Franz Ferdinand Carl Ludwig

Joseph Maria of Austria (1863–1914), whose death at the orders of the military society the Black Hand is considered one of the main triggers of the First World War.

28 *parole*: An oath or formal promise to return to one's captor if temporarily released.

39 *a bronze Leghorn*: A chicken from Leghorn (Livorno) in Tuscany valued as a 'layer'.

43 *prophet Elijah... fed by ravens*: A reference to the Biblical prophet Elijah, a miracle worker who lived in *c*.9th century BC Israel, and who advocated for the worship of Jehovah over Pagan gods and idols, such as Baal. 'Fed by ravens' is a reference to the story where God tells Elijah to flee from Israel, and to hide by a tributary of the Jordan, the Chorath, where he would be fed by ravens.

44 *No one could feel very strongly about Queen Anne*: Thought to be possibly due to sexist prejudice, Queen Anne (1665–1714, r. 1702–07) was often portrayed as dull, corpulent and uninterested in politics.

44 *Queen Anne's dead*: An idiom, generally taken to mean 'That's old news'.

46 *Quel type!*: 'What a sort!' (French).

51 *Mr Frederick Harrison*: Frederick Harrison (*c*.1854–1927) was an actor and theatre manager associated with the Theatre Royal Haymarket.

51 *The circumstances of our writing... Maude*: Included by Saki's sister in her posthumous collection of Saki's unpublished works, *The Square Egg and Other Sketches* (1924), this note is written by Charles Maude (1848–1927), Saki's friend and collaborator.

53 *escritoire*: A type of small writing desk with stationery drawers.

53   *Goodwood Week*: That is, during the annual festival at Goodwood Racecourse, established in 1802 on the estate of the Duke of Richmond in West Sussex.

55   *damask cheek*: A borrowing from Shakespeare's *Twelfth Night* (Act II, scene 4): 'But let concealment, like a worm i' the bud, feed on her damask cheek.'

56   *Catherine the Second of Russia*: A reference to Catherine the Great (1729–96, r. 1762–96), whose rule, considered a golden age for Russia, was authoritarian.

56   *Popery*: Anti-Catholic sentiment was still rife in many parts in England, arguably until the mid-twentieth century.

57   *Halma*: A board game played on a board with 256 squares, where counters leap one another in order to advance from one side to the other.

57   *Macedonian policy*: Having been largely ruled as part of the Ottoman Empire until 1912, Macedonia was captured by the Kingdom of Serbia in 1912, and was the subject of dispute between Serbia and Bulgaria.

58   *relict*: That is, widow.

59   *the nigger in the timber yard*: A dated and offensive figure of speech (usually 'in the woodpile') originating from the US – possibly from the concealment of escaped slaves on the Underground Railroad in timber-carrying carriages – and taken to mean a thing of great importance that hasn't been disclosed.

59   *dower house*: The house available to the widow of an estate owner.

61   *Queen Victoria's coronation*: Queen Victoria's coronation was on the 28th of June 1838.

62   *gymkhana*: A special day of horse racing and competitions.

62 *purple*: Rich, ostentatious, lavish.

65 *beat up*: That is, call up, summon.

65 *Cinderella*: More properly a 'Cinderella dance', a dancing party where guests must leave by midnight.

65 *Bradshaw at breakfast and a tea basket at Yeovil*: 'Bradshaw' refers to *Bradshaw's Guide*, the series of books of railway timetables. What Clare means is that Hortensia would send them packing as soon as she heard of the secret party.

65 *chafing dish*: A metal pan containing burning charcoal, used for cooking at the table.

66 *Salomé dances*: See Matthew 14:6: 'the daughter of Herodias danced before them, and pleased Herod.' This was interpreted by Oscar Wilde (1854–1900) in his 1891 play *Salomé* as 'the dance of the seven veils' – a play which was set to music by Richard Georg Strauss (1864–1949) as an opera, *Salome*, which premiered in 1905. Following this, a trend described as 'Salomania' sprung up, with a craze for performers of Salomé-inspired dancers at parties.

67 *St Martin's Summer*: That is, the feast day for St Martin of Tours (AD 316–397).

67 *East Wind*: In the Bible the East Wind is characterised as evil and as a bringer of destruction.

67 *Babes in the Wood… covering me with leaves*: A reference to the folktale known variously as *The Norfolk Tragedy* or *Babes in the Wood*, in which children wander in the woods until they die, and then birds cover them with leaves.

68 *Lulu Duchess of Dulverton*: The Duchess appears to be Saki's invention; she also appears in his short story 'The Treasure Ship' (first published in *Beasts and Super-Beasts* in 1914).

70 *going... the blind*: A reference to Luke 14:12: 'Then the master of the house being angry said to his servant, Go out quickly into the streets and lanes of the city, and bring in hither the poor, and the maimed, and the halt, and the blind.'

74 *coverts*: Thickets maintained for game to hide in.

74 *deservingly poor*: An archaic term, from a time when the poor were seen as something lesser, referring to someone who was deemed to be poor but with worthy or meritorious qualities.

79 *grass orphan*: An unusual phrase adapted from 'grass widow', a woman who lives apart from her husband or has been separated from her husband, either temporarily or permanently.

80 *mater*: 'Mother' (Latin).

81 *samovar*: A Russian tea urn heated with charcoals. (The name comes from the Russian, meaning 'self-boiler'.)

83 *a hen came in between them*: This scene is clearly an evolution of 'The Miracle Merchant', which was, in itself, an adaptation of Saki's short story 'The Hen' (first published in *Beasts and Super-Beasts* in 1914).

85 *nautch girl*: A dancer in South Asia (nautch was a type of dance common in the Court of the Mughal Empire).

85 *café chantant*: Literally 'singing café', these were a type of establishment associated with the Belle Époque in France, the music played at which was generally considered risqué.

87 *What does 'Bewegungslosigkeit' mean in English?*: 'Immobility' (German).

95 *kitchen lancers*: An energetic square dance, based on the quadrille.

99 *demi-mondaine*: Literally, 'half-worlder' (French), a Romantic-era term used to describe those considered to be of suspect moral or social character, one on the edges of society.

99 *Ibsen and Mrs Humphry Ward*: A reference to two writers – Henrik Johan Ibsen (1828–1906) and Mary Augusta Ward (1851–1920) – both of whom courted controversy for their writing and opinions.

100 *a rubber of bridge*: Rubber bridge is a form of bridge played between two competing pairs of players, who win by completing 'a rubber' (two winning games).

101 *worship of Mammon*: A Biblical character associated with wealth.

101 *Sabine women... borrowed by the Romans*: According to the Roman historian Livy (59 BC–AD 17), in the mid-8th century BC the ruler Romulus was concerned about sustaining the population of Rome, as the populace was predominantly male. He devised a plot, inviting inhabitants of the surrounding areas (including the Sabines) to visit, and kidnapped thirty women, killing the men accompanying them, and forcing the women to remain in the city. The incident is generally referred to as 'the Rape of the Sabine Women', and was the subject of many Renaissance paintings.

101 *Leda without the swan*: A reference to the Greek myth of Leda and the Swan, in which Zeus takes the form of a swan and seduces Leda, who goes on to bear children including Helen of Troy. Leda in a state of undress with the swan was a popular image for many artists.

107 *Sir Roger de Coverley*: An English country dance.

107 *up train*: That is, a train to London.

108 *It reminds me… eve of Waterloo*: A reference to the Duchess of Richmond's Ball, a ball held in Brussels on the 15th of June 1815, hosted by Charlotte Lennox, Duchess of Richmond (1768–1842), the night before the Battle of Quatre Bras (two days before the Battle of Waterloo). The Duke of Wellington (1769–1852) wanted to give spies the impression that the British forces were not afraid of any impending attacks, so the ball went ahead in the face of suggestions that the French were about to invade. It soon became clear that the army would have to leave to fight the following morning, and the ball took on a rather sombre air, with families uncertain whether they would see their husbands and fathers again.

114 *jerry-built*: That is, shoddily built – used to describe things that are built with poor materials and by poor workmanship.

117 *Cheap Jack store*: 'Cheap Jack' usually refers to a travelling salesman who offers items at an inflated price and expects to be bartered with; by extension, Agatha suggests Mrs Vulpy is common and of lower worth than she at first seems.

122 *Plymouth Brethren*: A low-church, nonconformist group which teaches that the Bible is the utmost source of wisdom, above any Church figure of authority.

122 *Non je ne marcherai pas*: 'No, I won't walk' (French), presumably the lyrics to a song.

127 *board schools*: A type of elementary school which was overseen by a school board.

127 *I should insist on its being done in camera*: That is, in private; a legal term referring to proceedings taking place in a judge's private chambers rather than in open court.

132 Your sleeve's in the butter, miss: Here there are clear echoes of 'The Miracle Merchant' again (see also note to p. 83).

134 The 3.20 up or the 4.15 down, miss: Perhaps René was mistaken when he spoke of a 3.15 up train (see second note to p. 107).

136 sauve qui peut: 'Run for your life' (French).

137 gorgon: In Greek mythology, three sisters – most famously Medusa – who had snakes for hair and whose gaze turned people to stone.

137 rake: That is, a libertine (possibly also a pun on farming).

137 grass-widowhood: (See first note to p. 79.)

145 harelip: Another term for a cleft lip; the detail is reflective of an unpleasant dismissal of those with physical disabilities or birth defects that was common at the time.

147 The Christian Apologists: Presumably Ludovic means apologetics, the branch of Christian theology that defends the faith against disbelief through argument and essay (although perhaps mistaking the name for comic effect).

147 taken things betimes: That is, he is early, ahead of time.

149 Some poet... full of sorrow: A reference to 'Ode to a Nightingale' (1819) by John Keats (1795–1821).

149 The ghost scene from Hamlet: That is, Act I, scene 5.

150 it was very like Maeterlinck: Maurice Maeterlinck (1862–1949) was a Belgian playwright who was renowned for his early preternatural and supernatural plays.

150 Whoever really... Maxim Gorky: There has been fierce debate over the years as to whether Shakespeare really wrote all of his own plays. Maxim Gorky (1868–1936) was a Russian writer who was best known for the social realism in his writings. (Perhaps also a nod to the dual authorship of 'The Watched Pot'.)

154 P. & O. steamer: Formerly the Peninsular and Oriental Steam Navigation Company, P. & O. for short, now generally known as P&O.

156 the reign of the Georges: George I (1660–1727) ascended to the throne in 1714, and was followed by George II (1683–1760, r. 1727–60), George III (1738–1820, r. 1760–1820) and George IV (1762–1830, r. 1820–30), so 'the reign of the Georges' was 1714–1830.

156 the Blue Danube: The Danube is the main river flowing through Hungary. The addition of 'blue' alludes to a well-known 1866 waltz by Johann Strauss II (1825–99), commonly known in English as 'The Blue Danube'.

156 Debrett: John Debrett (1753–1822), compiler of the guides and lists of the peerage, *Debrett's*.

161 There's a proverb… happens next: Presumably a reference to the idiom about 'the cat that got the cream' (interestingly, this is another recycled joke, this time from 'The Way to the Dairy', a short story published in *The Chronicles of Clovis* in 1911.

163 black Minorcas: A type of domestic chicken.

164 Omar Khayyám: A reference to the Persian poet Omar Khayyám (1048–1131), who is best known for the 1859 translation of his *Rubáiyát* by Edward FitzGerald (1809–83). Mrs Vulpy's meaning is unclear, although, given that she goes on to talk about peacocks, perhaps Saki has in mind the luxurious edition of the book commissioned by the rare book dealers Harry Southeran, completed in 1911, which had a gilt cover adorned with three peacocks with bejewelled tails. (See also the biographical note on p. 185 for more information on Saki's interest in the *Rubáiyát*.)

164 Return of the prodigal... fatted calf: A reference to the Biblical story of the Prodigal Son (see Luke 15:11–32). The return of the prodigal son is celebrated with a feast with a fatted calf at the centre.

165 chows: A breed of dog.

165 Inkerman: A reference to the Battle of Inkerman, fought on the 5th of November 1854 during the Crimean War.

171 Heidsieck: Piper Heidsieck, a brand of Champagne.

173 Moselle: A white wine produced in three countries through which the river Moselle (or Mosel) runs.

A Brief Biographical
Note on Saki

Hector Hugh Munro, better known by his pen name, Saki (a name which is thought to be borrowed from the cupbearer in *The Rubáiyát of Omar Khayyám*), was born on the 18th of December 1870 in Myanmar (then Burma) to Charles Munro, an Inspector General in the Burma Police, and Mary Mercer, the daughter of a Rear Admiral.

Mary died just two years after Saki was born, and his father moved the family to England, where they were sent to Barnstaple in Devon to be brought up by their strict grandmother and two aunts – characters who crop up throughout his oeuvre. 'Aunt Tom', writes Saki's sister Ethel in her biography of her brother, 'was a colossal humbug, and never knew it. The other aunt, Augusta, is the one who, more or less, is depicted in 'Sredni Vashtar' (one of Saki's stories).

Saki was sent to school in Exmouth, and then, aged fifteen, to Bedford Grammar School. It wasn't until 1896 that he moved to London, hoping to make a career by his pen.

In 1900, he published his first book, *The Rise of the Russian Empire*, a historical study which proved rather unpopular, but was considered very well researched and written.

He was introduced (by some Devon friends) to the illustrator Francis Carruthers Gould, who 'discovered' him – according to J.A. Spender, the editor of the *Westminster Gazette* at the time, 'I have a clear recollection of Gould's bringing him to my room at the office somewhere about the year 1900 and starting then and there on a discussion of articles which the one was to write and the other to illustrate.'

Following the great success of *The Westminster Alice*, Saki placed many stories with *The Westminster Gazette*, many of which were illustrated by Gould, and he started to get a name for his satirical style. In 1902 he took up a position for *The Morning Post* as a foreign correspondent in the Balkans and, later, in Russia, but continued to publish short stories in *The Morning Post*, *The Bystander* and *The Westminster Gazette* in the mean time.

In 1908 he returned to live in London, and also bought a house in the Surrey Hills, where Ethel lived as his tenant, and continued to publish his short stories.

When World War I broke out, Saki was 43, and therefore wasn't called up to fight (the Military Service Act, passed in January 1916, imposed conscription on all single men aged 18–41, with a few exemptions), but volunteered for service anyway, eventually becoming Lance Sergeant in the 22nd Battalion of the Royal Fusiliers.

Sadly, he was killed by a German sniper during the Battle of the Ancre while he and his company sheltered; his last words were reportedly, 'Put that bloody cigarette out!'

After his death, Ethel destroyed most of his papers (quite a common practice at the time), so most of the personal details about Saki in the public realm come from her biography, which was published in *The Square Egg* in 1924.

However, some of the details which might have been struck from the record were not expunged by Ethel's pen, and she did not seek to suppress rumours that Saki was homosexual (which was illegal during his lifetime). Instead of addressing such rumours, at the end of her biography she states, 'I have not touched upon his social life, visits to country-house parties, etc., because they would not be of interest to the general reader.'

Although Saki has no known grave and no archive of personal information, his legacy is enormous – excluding the few serialised sketches he wrote for various papers which were not later collected and published in volume form (notably *The Not-So Stories* and *The Political Jungle Book* series), his bibliography includes a full-length play, two one-act plays, a historical study, two novels (besides *The Westminster Alice*, which is normally seen more as a series of sketches than a novella) and around a hundred and thirty short stories. His reputation still shows no signs of waning, and he is considered an undisputed master of the short-story genre.

MORE CLASSIC THEATRE FROM
RENARD PRESS

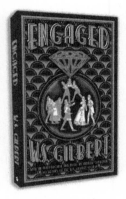

ISBN: 9781913724061
Paperback
£7.99 • 160pp

ISBN: 9781913724672
Paperback
£6.99 • 144pp

ISBN: 9781913724429
Paperback
£7.99 • 128pp

ISBN: 9781913724658
Paperback
£7.99 • 256pp

ISBN: 9781913724054
Paperback with gold foil
£7.99 • 128pp

ISBN: 9781913724368
Paperback with gold foil
£7.99 • 96pp

DISCOVER THE FULL COLLECTION AT
WWW.RENARDPRESS.COM